The Urban Astronomer

Other Related Wiley Science Editions

The Starry Room, by Fred Schaaf

Seven Ideas That Shook the Universe, by Bryan D. Anderson and Nathan Speilberg

The Starflight Handbook: A Pioneer's Guide to Interstellar Travel, by Eugene Mallove and Gregory Matloff

Planets Beyond: Discovering the Outer Solar System, by Mark Littmann

Starsailing, by Louis Friedman

The Search for Extraterrestrial Intelligence, by Thomas R. McDonough

Space: The Next Twenty-Five Years, by Thomas R. McDonough

Seeing the Sky: 100 Projects, Activities, and Explorations in Astronomy, by Fred Schaaf

Touring the Universe through Binoculars: A Complete Astronomer's Guidebook, by Philip S. Harrington

Levitating Trains and Kamikaze Genes: Technological Literacy for the 1990s, by Richard P. Brennan

The Beauty of Light, by Ben Bova

The Urban Astronomer
A Practical Guide for Observers in Cities and Suburbs

Gregory L. Matloff

with drawings by Constance Bangs

John Wiley & Sons, Inc.
NEW YORK • CHICHESTER • BRISBANE • TORONTO • SINGAPORE

To all those who have sought the stars
and to those who will reach for them
in years to come.

*In recognition of the importance of preserving what has been written, it is a
policy of John Wiley & Sons, Inc., to have books of enduring value published in
the United States printed on acid-free paper, and we exert our best efforts to
that end.*

Library of Congress Cataloging-in-Publication Data

Matloff, Gregory L.
    The urban astronomer : a practical guide for observers
in cities and suburbs / by Gregory L. Matloff : drawings by
Constance Bangs.
        p.   cm.—(Wiley science editions)
    Includes bibliographical references and index.
    ISBN 0-471-53142-1 (alk. paper).—ISBN 0-471-53143-X (pbk. :
alk. paper)
    1. Astronomy—Amateurs' manuals. 2. Astronomy—Observers'
manuals. I. Title. II. Series.
QB63.M43   1991
523—dc20   91-9316

Printed in the United States of America
91 92 10 9 8 7 6 5 4 3 2 1

Preface

But see! Where Daphne wondering mounts on high
Above the clouds, above the starry sky
Eternal beauties grace the shining scene.
Fields ever fresh and groves ever green!
—Alexander Pope, *The Fourth Pastoral or Daphne*
(1709)

At first glance, the concept of an "urban astronomer" might seem contradictory. In the city, open space is at a premium and street-lights are everywhere. To do real astronomy, you might think that a trip to the country is in order. Only there, amid the comforting darkness of the lonely rural nights, are most of the stellar denizens of the evening sky visible in all their splendor.

Most guides to amateur astronomy are, in fact, produced with the rural skyviewer at heart. The skycharts presented in these ex-cellent works show thousands of stars, the outline of our galaxy's local spiral arm (the Milky Way), and many objects far more dis-tant than the farthest star in our galaxy.

Modern urbanites are probably less knowledgeable about viewing the sky than were many people from less sophisticated cultures. Among the major goals of any urban astronomy venture is the education of the public to the point at which scientific method, controlled experimentation, and dispassionate analysis can be appreciated. Keeping this in mind, I have included many sky activities in this book that can be enjoyed by a novice astrono-mer from an urban location.

Amateur astronomy from an urban setting can help renew our ties with the cosmos. In this era of growing urbanization and glo-bal cooperation, as humanity works to repair Earth's environment and begins to turn its attention to Mars, efforts to renew our cosmic roots will be important. In this respect the contributions of the individual urban astronomer can be quite significant. There is another compelling reason to observe the skies from the city—it is fun!

My own introduction to urban astronomy came in 1958, when I received a 3.5-inch diameter reflecting telescope from my parents as a thirteenth-birthday gift. I practiced first on terrestrial objects (smokestacks, buildings, etc.) a few miles distant from my Brooklyn observing location. The first thing I noticed was that the image through an astronomical telescope, unlike the image through binoculars, is inverted or upside down. But it was when I pointed the telescope at a suitable sky target that my fate was sealed. My mother would have liked me to pursue business or the law. My father would probably have liked me to follow in his footsteps and become a dentist. When I looked at the crescent Moon through low power in my Sky Scope on that balmy spring evening in 1958, I knew that for me it was the stars or it was nothing!

Magnified 35 times, the Moon hung suspended and shimmered in the hazy Brooklyn skies. I seemed transported from the third-story roof on my father's building to deep space. Never before, and rarely since, have I heard so plainly the music of the spheres.

As I gazed, I noticed the enhanced brightness of our planet's one natural satellite. As my eye adjusted to the image, I could clearly see the terminator—the line between sunlight and darkness on the Moon's visual face. Soon, the long shadows of craters and mountains became visible. I already knew that some of these mountains rivaled Mount Everest.

I of course could not know that, less than a dozen years later, I would breathlessly follow the epic flight of two men in a flimsy craft as they descended to land in one of the Moon's large lava flows, or maria, during the mission of Apollo 11. It was evident, even through the turbulent skies of Brooklyn, how some of the early telescopic astronomers thought erroneously that these dry lunar plains were actually water-filled ocean basins.

Soon, I turned my attention to the naked-eye planets. Mars showed a ruddy disk with some surface detail and a hint of white polar cap under high magnification. Jupiter, "the King of the Planets," was spectacular with its multihued gas bands and clearly visible retinue of four large "Galilean" satellites. Also clearly visible, under moderate magnification, was the Great Red Spot, that mysterious and chaotic disturbance in Jupiter's clouds. The Great Red Spot is so large that it could very easily engulf Earth.

Although I could never discern surface detail on mysterious Venus, I often observed our cloud-wracked nearest planetary neighbor. Because Venus is closer to the Sun than is Earth, its phases are clearly visible to the earthbound observer.

If Jupiter is the king of the planets, Saturn clearly ranks as a pretender to the throne. We now know, thanks to the far-flying and intrepid *Voyager* robots, that all of the gas giant planets (Jupiter, Saturn, Uranus, and Neptune) have ring systems. Only the rings of Saturn, however, are clearly visible in a small telescope. On clear nights from New York City, I have often observed Cassini's division, a gap in Saturn's rings.

I was a fortunate young New Yorker because my parents owned a small summer house in the Hamptons. I was able to escape the summer swelter. Of course, I brought my precious Sky Scope with me to the sands of Long Island. In the clearer seaside nights, I was able to see the Milky Way. This enormous structure is invisible (to the unassisted eye) from most urban settings that I have observed from. Also, during the middle and late summer, I became acquainted with Messier 31, the spiral galaxy in the constellation Andromeda. The Andromeda Galaxy is very similiar to our Milky Way.

I stayed up late during the summer to view meteors. I had more success with that effort than in my attempts to observe the early *Sputnik* and *Explorer* satellites from Long Island, Brooklyn, or the house my parents would soon purchase in the borough of Queens. It was not until the early 1960s that I had better luck with the larger and brighter *Echo* orbital balloons.

That winter, in the driveway of the new house in Queens, I continued my evening journeys into the stellar immensity. I found that even urban streetlights could not greatly diminish a recurrent spectacle of the winter skies—Messier 42, the Orion nebula. In this beautiful bluish green dust cloud, infant stars are being "hatched" even as we watch. Billions of years ago, Earth and our entire Solar System must have originated in a similar patch of interstellar dust and gas.

As well as being the celestial home of this nebulosity, the constellation Orion has some of the brightest and most colorful stars in the heavens. Like many young amateurs, I soon became an aficionado of star colors and sought out those binary stars visible with my equipment.

This early passion would serve me well. I would study physics in college and play a small role in the development of the first orbiting astronomical observatories—the OAO project. Later, better educated and somewhat older, I would spend a year at a major observatory. Over many more years, I would acquire a Ph.D. in atmospheric science, consult for NASA, teach, and become an expert in the infant discipline of interstellar travel.

Since late 1986, I have directed an urban astronomy program for the Department of Parks and Recreation of the City of New York. I have been struck by the fascination of typical urban dwellers regarding the Moon, the Sun, and those planets, constellations, and deep-sky objects that are visible in the gloomy urban skies. Youngsters in particular seem to be fascinated by the heavens perhaps because they have grown up in the space age or perhaps because of some more obscure reason. Whatever the motivation, I have discovered that their enthusiasm about the universe can be channeled into relatively painless training in computer skills and other important disciplines.

This book is designed for use by the intelligent urbanite with an interest in astronomy. If it sparks your interest to participate in some of the activities described or to read further in the references listed, it has succeeded in its goal.

I would not have been able to complete *The Urban Astronomer* without the support and assistance of my wife, Constance Bangs. Connie's chapter frontispiece drawings grace these pages and, I hope, enrich the material. Members of the Amateur Astronomers Association of New York have also been of invaluable aid. The photographs of the urban night sky were, in fact, provided by John Pazmino, a long-time member of that organization. Discussions with my long-time collaborator, MIT science writer Dr. Eugene Mallove, are also gratefully acknowledged.

My father, Simon, has also been most supportive; I am sorry that my mother, Eudice, did not live to see the finished product. Without their encouragement at an early age, I would not have been able to consider an astronomical career.

Connie's parents, Ernest and Isabelle, have also been a great help. I am particularly thankful for my access to Ernest's library in Ithaca, New York (where the skies are often very clear).

Numerous employees in the Department of Parks and Recreation of the City of New York have been very helpful in implementing my program. Among these are Commissioner Betsy Gottbaum, Assistant Commissioner Bill Castro, and Former Commissioner Henry Stern.

This book could not have been produced without the encouragement of my literary agent, Richard Curtis. I also appreciate the direction of my editor at John Wiley & Sons, David Sobel, and the able assistance of Nancy Woodruff and Kate Bradford. In addition, Laura Cleveland and the staff at WordCrafters Editorial Services Inc., also were instrumental in generating the final version of this manuscript.

Gregory L. Matloff

Brooklyn, New York

Contents

CHAPTER 6
Unusual Stars   101

Introduction: A Historical Perspective

I heard what was said of the universe,
Heard it and heard it of several thousand years;
It is middling well as far as it goes—but is that all?
This is the city and I am one of the citizens.
Whatever interests the rest interests me, politics,
    wars, markets, newspapers, schools
The mayor and councils, banks, tariffs, steamships,
    factories, stocks, real estate and personal estate.
—Walt Whitman, *Song of Myself* (1881)

In the busy life of most modern city dwellers, nothing seems more irrelevant than the study of astronomy. Most urbanites rise early in the morning, take some form of mass conveyance to work or school, and sit at their desks until noon. Then, after a short break for lunch, they resume their professional activities.

As they leave the office at 5 P.M., they may briefly notice the beauties of the twilight or the mysterious lights in the evening sky. Most people know that the brightest of these evening sky objects, the Moon, is our world's natural satellite and has been visited by a number of human and robot explorers. But how many can identify Sirius, the brightest star in the sky, or the naked-eye planets from an urban setting? Four of these—Venus, Mars, Jupiter, and Saturn—are visible even from the lamp-lit streets of New York.

One reason for our relative ignorance of the night sky is the ever-present streetlight. In banishing darkness and enhancing the evening efficiency and security of the urban street, we have cut the modern urban dweller off from the cosmos.

If inhabitants of the ancient world were dropped into the wilderness without a compass, they would have a considerable survival advantage over modern sophisticates. Before the invention of the streetlight, most people had at least a passing acquaintance with the patterns of stellar constellations in the night sky and could easily use these to locate the North Star. Since the North Star always retains its position close to and above Earth's north pole, this object is an excellent navigational marker. If you are ever lost at night in the woods without a compass and the weather is clear, you can easily navigate if you can locate Polaris, the present-day North Star.

You can do this by first locating the Big Dipper, the most familiar arrangement of stars in the night sky. Then, as shown in the star charts in Appendix 6, you can follow an imaginary line between the two end stars in the cup of the Big Dipper. If you extend this line, the first bright star you come to is Polaris, which is also the tip of the Little Dipper. Polaris is always very close to Earth's geographic north pole. If you face this star, north is directly in front of you; south is behind you; east is to your right; and west is on the left.

Civilization and astronomy coevolved, in fact. As Neolithic (late Stone Age) humans began to settle into agricultural communities more than 7,000 years ago, the need for calendar markers developed. When were the optimum times to plant and harvest the crops and to plan the feast days for thanking the earth and sky gods? When were the official beginnings of the annual seasons?

These questions occurred not to wide-eyed astronomers leading the lives of hermits in their mountain retreats, but to those very people who conducted the business and politics of the day. To the farm owners, mayors, and animal husbanders of Jericho, Malta, and other early settlements, the calendar was a matter of economic life and death.

Somewhere back in the mists of these preliterate times, a single genius or group of observant people noticed the regularity of motions of the brightest lights in the celestial firmament—the Sun and the Moon. On every nonovercast day, they watched the Sun rise in the east, reach its highest point in the sky at noon, and then descend toward its setting point in the west. During the warm summer months, the hours of daylight are long and the temperature is consequently high. The Sun is high in the sky. In the cold northern winters, the sun never ventures very far above the horizon. Days are short and temperatures are low.

At night, they observed the goddess of the evening sky—the Moon—repeat her eternal dance across the sky. Also rising in the east and setting in the west, the Moon's phases increase from new to waxing crescent to half to waxing gibbous and finally to full, when the Moon's face is fully lit. Then, the Moon decreases through waning gibbous, half, waning crescent, and, once again, new. The cycle of lunar phases repeats endlessly, with a period of one lunar month.

Early calendar astronomers devoted a great deal of time to reconciling the 365-day annual cycle of the Sun and the 29-day lunar month. Because of the divine nature of these sky orbs (from the point of view of many ancient peoples), calendar studies were a matter not just of science and economics, but of theological interest as well.

The names of the ancient men and women who carefully gathered data about the apparent motions of the Sun and Moon are lost to us forever. But, perhaps surprisingly, some of their observational instruments still remain.

A few thousand years after the foundations of the first agricultural settlements and before the start of the classical civilizations of the ancient world, humans in parts of northern Europe passed through the Megalithic stage. Immense stone monuments were raised, many of which remain to the present day.

About 5,000 years ago, inhabitants of the villages on or near Salisbury Plain in Britain erected the first stones of Stonehenge. For more than 1,000 years, they improved the structure and added to it. Then, mysteriously, they abandoned it. Legend had it that King Arthur's magician Merlin had raised the stone circle by magic. It was a modern astronomer, Professor Gerald Hawkins, armed with a digital computer, who proved almost beyond doubt that Stonehenge was an ancient observatory built to keep track of the Sun and Moon.

But surely the vast effort devoted to the original Neolithic Stonehenge was for more than just calendar improvement. A simple set of wooden markers—like the vertical shaft, or gnomon, of the sundial—would be sufficient for routine solar and lunar observations.

As Hawkins and other astronomers have speculated, the reason for the construction of the elaborate Neolithic observatories may be the prediction of those formerly feared celestial events—eclipses. Eclipses of the Sun occur when the Moon passes between the Sun and the observer; eclipses of the Moon, when Earth passes between the Sun and the Moon.

To ancient people, of course, the exact cause of eclipses was a mystery. Calendar scholars may have recognized that they could enhance their power and economic status by using their equipment to predict eclipses of the Sun and Moon.

The penalty for these early astronomical entrepreneurs was quite severe in case of false prediction. According to tradition, two early Chinese astronomers were executed when they mispredicted a solar eclipse and thereby embarrassed the local king.

One can easily imagine the power of the priest–astronomer during this stage of civilization: The people are ushered from their villages to take their appointed places by the sky temple. As the bright, sunny day progresses, a priest tells them that a monstrous dragon will attempt to devour the Sun. Only if they promise to atone for their sins, pay their taxes on time, and so on, will the source of heat and light be released by the celestial monster. The people laugh—they have heard it all before. Suddenly, the sky begins to mysteriously darken as musicians begin to beat drums. The laughter ceases as the darkness deepens. In unison, the priests begin to chant.

The people prostrate themselves. They tear their hair and clothes and promise anything—if the Sun will only return. At the peak of totality, the chief priest–astronomer reassures the people that they are winning and that the monster is defeated. As the sky begins to brighten, the people stare in wonder. Birds rise again from their nocturnal roosts. The short, terrible night ends, and the power of the priest–astronomer, the clergy, and the tax collectors has been reaffirmed. In a few years, during another solar eclipse or a less dramatic eclipse of the Moon at night, the ritual will be repeated.

Once again, the major beneficiary of astronomical knowledge was the sophisticated urbanite—the broker of power and wealth. After the invention of writing and the spread of literacy, eclipse prediction was no longer the mystery that it had formerly been. If astronomers were to maintain their favored lifestyles, a new sky cult was required.

In the period of Babylon's flowering, about 3,000 years ago, such a sky cult developed. Although motions of the chief sky gods—the Sun and Moon—were predictable, a number of bright "wandering" stars had more complex paths. These naked-eye planets—Mercury, Venus, Mars, Jupiter, and Saturn—seemed to move in complex tracks across the sky. Sometimes, they would even seem to loop backward, or retrograde. Like the Sun and Moon, these wanderers seemed to be confined to a narrow band, called the *ecliptic*. The major stellar patterns along the ecliptic made up the 12 constellations of the *zodiac*.

In the new celestial religions of the classical world, the wandering stars were identified with the gods and goddesses of the pantheon. Jupiter, "the King of the Gods," was marked by its bright constancy, and Saturn, with its comparatively slow track across the sky, was identified with the god of time. Fleet Mercury was the god of commerce and the messenger of the other celestial deities. Mars, "the Red Planet," was identified with the war god because of its sanguine complexion. Bright (fickle) Venus, sometimes an evening star and sometimes a morning star, was identified with the ancient goddess of love.

No crude stone circles for these Bronze Age astronomers! Instead, some of the most monumental structures ever constructed in the ancient world—the ziggurats of the Mesopotamian cities—were dedicated to the observation of the wandering sky gods. None of these structures, with their tapering towers and spiraling paths to the summit, still stands. The grandest of the ziggurats, however, is immortalized in the Bible as the Tower of Babel.

Ascending nightly to the summits of their artificial mountains, the Bronze Age astronomers would observe the position of the visible planets with sophisticated (for the time) pointing instruments and record the planetary positions in reference to the fixed stars. These 3,000-year-old written records have greatly aided scholars in constructing the modern vision of our solar system.

Of course, pure and disinterested knowledge was not the main goal of the Babylonian sky observers. Because they were observing not mere worlds but (in their view) celestial deities, the observations would translate into predictions and great worldly power. The Chaldean sky observers had invented the art of astrology.

For millenia, many rulers would not make a move without consulting the court astrologer. The timing of military action, business dealings, and love affairs would depend to a large degree upon the positions of the naked-eye planets in the horoscopes of the powerful.

For more than 2,000 years, however, it was the very rare astronomer in the western world who never cast a horoscope. Even though this strange marriage between astronomy and astrology might have been discomforting to many ancient, medieval, and Renaissance scholars of the heavens, financial necessity was a more powerful motivating force.

At the dawn of the Age of Science, Tycho Brahe and Galileo observed the planets while theoreticians such as Copernicus and Kepler attempted to understand their motions. Inductive studies, typified by careful and repeated measurements, replaced the purely deductive approach of the ancient philosophers.

Earth shrank and shifted position. No longer was it stationary at the center of creation. It became another world, like Mercury, Venus, and the rest. Like the celestial wanderers, Earth pursued an endless closed ellipse (or orbit) around the Sun. And the Sun itself was not the center of creation, but was a mere speck of star dust amidst the glory of the Milky Way Galaxy.

More than three centuries ago, that brilliant eccentric Isaac Newton was born in England. He was destined to combine the naked-eye observations of Tycho Brahe, the telescopic and theoretical work of Galileo, and the insights of Copernicus and Kepler and create the new disciplines of calculus and Newtonian physics. The modern world was created by his magnificent synthesis. The modern factory, skyscraper, auto, subway, airplane, television, power station, and rocket—essentially all technology rests upon "Newton's Revolution." Astronomy, as "the Mother of Physics," had helped create the modern world!

We seem to be at a branch point in human evolution where past ways of looking at the world and at one another have increasingly less relevance. At least some of the responsibility for the present-day "paradigm shift" rests with physicists and astronomers of the early twentieth century.

It is paradoxical that the work of these people has resulted in a civilization that is technologically more isolated from nature and the cosmos than any before. This is particularly ironic in light of the personal philosophies of these men and women, many of whom were interested in illuminating the natural fabric they were part of, not dominating it.

A few examples from different fields of endeavor will serve to show how far our technology has brought us from oneness with the universe. The examples that follow involve the farmer and the navigator.

In past epochs, nothing was more sky-oriented than the work of the farmer. The rising and setting positions of the Sun and the highest point in the sky that the Sun reaches on a particular day were significant calendar points for the sowing and gathering of crops. From the point of view of an early farmer in the Northern Hemisphere, the agricultural year begins on the first day of spring, when the lengths of day and night are equal (the vernal equinox) and the Sun is directly above the Celestial Equator (the projection of Earth's equator in the sky). The days are lengthening then; the soil is warming. It is time to prepare the ground for the first seeds.

By the summer solstice in June, when the Sun reaches its farthest point north of the Celestial Equator, seeds should be in the soil to take advantage of the warmth and increased precipitation. The harvest season is signaled by the autumnal equinox in September, when the Sun crosses the Celestial Equator and once again heads south.

When the winter solstice occurs in December, the days are beginning to lengthen. Even though warm days are still months in the future, the farmer can rejoice. The Sun is returning, and the earth will once again brim with life.

The modern farmer need never look at the sky. Excellent weather forecasts can be obtained from radio and television, and computerized projections of growing season length from a host of agricultural services. Agricultural planning is now the province of the specialist; the folk wisdom of earlier farmers and their knowledge of celestial cycles are things of the past.

Shipboard navigators used to know the skies very well. From the time of the Phoenicians to the era of the clipper ships of the nineteenth century, ship position was determined by observation of the Sun, the planets, and a number of "navigational stars" using increasingly sophisticated sighting instruments.

For some preliterate sailors, notably the Polynesians, star positions and prevailing wind patterns were passed from one generation of navigators to another by epic poetry committed to memory. Much later, organizations such as the U.S. Naval Observatory were devoted to gathering star data for the use of the navigator.

Today, except on spacecraft and military ships and aircraft, few navigators regularly practice the ancient art of "shooting the stars." Instead, they are masters of the computer and the radio network. They may instead triangulate radio beams emanating from a number of fixed locations or detect signals from an artificial constellation of Earth-orbiting navigational satellites.

Technology seems to have distanced us from the heavens in our day-to-day practical activities. But at the same time, humans are moving into the skies. People are already permanent inhabitants of the heavens aboard Space Station *Mir*. Barring catastrophe, we can safely predict cities in orbit and on the Moon, bases on Mars, and greenhouse-equipped liners that cycle endlessly between worlds. Many citizens of our urban culture are excited by these developments and seek to participate in them. Urban astronomy is a focusing force for their interest.

CHAPTER 1

Are Those Lights in the Skies Stars?

Jupiter shall emerge, be patient, watch again
    another night, the Pleiades shall emerge,
They are immortal, all those stars both silvery and
    golden shall shine out again,
The great stars and the little ones shall shine out
    again, they endure,
The vast immortal suns and the long-enduring
    pensive moons shall again shine.
—Walt Whitman, *Year of Meteors* (1859–1860)

One major problem facing the urban astronomer is finding a way to actually view the heavens! Sky visibility from the urban setting is problematical due to a number of factors including streetlights, automobile headlights, and smog. Although tall buildings can serve as urban observatories, they can also obscure and therefore significantly reduce the amount of sky visible to a ground-based observer. Seasonal variations are also pronounced in the urban setting. When more stars are visible during the clear skies of winter, the outdoor temperatures are less comfortable in many cities.

The urban astronomer must also contend with a problem possibly unique to our time of increased urbanization. If he or she finally succeeds in locating an urban location of comparatively low light level, one that is also isolated from buildings that obscure the sky, the darkness and isolation of the site might be scary. The nocturnal habits of the mugger and the drug dealer have not helped the cause of urban astronomy!

The Flight of a Photon

We can gain some insight into the frustrations of the urban astronomer by considering the plight of a typical photon of light from its point of view. Spawned in a star in the Andromeda Spiral Galaxy, our photon began its voyage to Earth when the ancestors of humanity had not yet descended from the trees. Fire was more than two million years in our future, not to mention clothing and language.

As humanity slowly evolved, eons passed on Earth. From the photon's relativistic viewpoint, however, the entire journey took less time than a Sunday outing on the freeway (assuming no gridlock, of course). Somewhere en route, our photon narrowly missed a black hole and was almost warped into an entirely different sector of space-time.

For most of its long journey, however, our photon was far from the gravitational fields of black holes, stars, and other massive denizens of the universe. Instead, it cruised in relative isolation through the near-perfect vacuum of the interstellar medium.

The interstellar medium, that vast desert between the stars, is not completely empty. Photons of light traveling through it interact occasionally with the atoms and dust grains found between the stars.

After its narrow escape from the clutch of the black hole, our photon could not even pause for breath before it and its relatives in the Andromeda Stream were affected by interstellar reddening. Many of its bluer cousins were scattered away by grains of interstellar dust between the Andromeda Galaxy and Earth. Other photons vanished into the maw of hungry atoms—their colors (or wavelengths) happened to exactly match the absorption bands of characteristic atoms in the interstellar medium. (The energy of the absorbed photons goes to excite or heat the atoms in the interstellar medium. The colors of the absorbed photons are missing from the spectra of starlight reaching Earth. The missing spectral regions are called *absorption bands*.)

Finally, our intrepid photon and its surviving companions enter Earth's outer atmosphere. Traveling at 186,300 miles per second, the photon stream reaches Earth's surface in less than 1/1000 of a second.

But there are some more casualties along the way. First, many of our photon's high-energy counterparts—those in the gamma- and X-ray ranges of the electromagnetic spectrum—are absorbed by atoms in Earth's ionosphere. Closer to the ground, hungry ozone molecules devour many of the remaining ultraviolet photons.

Some of the photon's visible counterparts are scattered out by interaction with atoms in the lower atmosphere, or troposphere. Others bounce off clouds or, in the case of infrared photons, are absorbed by water vapor or carbon dioxide in Earth's troposphere.

Finally, our photon and a few companions make it to "the big time." They enter the city from above and zero in on the light-hungry mirror of an urban astronomer. Then, just as they are about to enter the telescope tube, the streetlights go on! The whole, incredible journey has been in vain as the information content of the messengers from Andromeda is buried in local luminosity.

Of course, our photon voyager is a figment of the imagination. Fortunately, the universe produces so many photons that the loss of most of them to black holes, interstellar reddening, a host of atmospheric effects, and streetlights is less than tragic. However, the problems of urban observing are genuine.

The fate of starlight in even the most pristine atmosphere cannot be considered to be simple. To illuminate some of the vagaries of seeing through Earth's atmosphere, we return to our photon and reconsider the last 1/1000 of a second of its long journey as it plunges into Earth's upper atmosphere.

It is very fortunate for all life on Earth that our photon's high-energy (gamma-ray and X-ray) relatives are absorbed high in the ionosphere, more than 50 miles above our heads. These small bullets of high-energy light are very penetrating. They are quite capable of disrupting the internal structure of living cells, causing cancerlike radiation sickness. Most people working with X-rays (doctors, dentists, some industrial technicians) are required to limit their annual dosage and wear protective gear. Unlike X-rays, which cannot penetrate bone, higher-energy gamma rays can affect the function of the bone marrow and thus the normal functioning of an organism's immune system.

About 20 miles above the surface, the surviving photons from the Andromeda Stream encounter the stratospheric ozone layer.

Ozone, a fragile molecule constructed of three oxygen atoms, is closely related to the molecular oxygen that we breathe. The much more stable oxygen molecule consists of two oxygen atoms. Human-produced chemical pollution is thought to be responsible for disruption to the stratospheric ozone layer currently occurring over the Southern Hemisphere.

Ozone is a good absorber of ultraviolet. If the damage to the stratospheric ozone layer proves to be irreversible, the flux of ultraviolet light reaching the surface will increase. The incidence of skin cancers in fair-skinned people will consequently increase as well.

Farther down, less than 6 miles from the surface, the surviving photons from space encounter the troposphere, the lowest atmospheric layer. The troposphere contains most of Earth's weather. Water and ice clouds reflect many of the photons back into space. The denser atmosphere near the surface will preferentially scatter blue light in all directions, which accounts for the sky's color.

In the lower atmosphere, we find the so-called greenhouse gases. These molecules, which include carbon dioxide and water vapor, are good absorbers of infrared radiation.

When light emitted by the Sun reaches Earth's surface, some is reflected back to space and some is absorbed. The absorbed solar energy will heat the surface and later be reemitted as infrared. An increased abundance of infrared-absorbing greenhouse gases will result in additional atmospheric heating. Carbon dioxide, which is a product of all combustion, may result in increased temperatures on Earth in the early twenty-first century.

If our photon had made the much quicker (8-minute) hop from the Sun, which is a mere (relatively speaking) 92.5 million miles away, it might have been affected by another atmospheric phenomenon—refraction. When light enters Earth's atmosphere from the near-vacuum conditions of space, it slows down from 186,300 miles per second to 186,248 miles per second.

For light rays nonperpendicular to the surface, particularly rays near the horizon, the slight velocity change results in a slight bending in the light ray's path. Light from the Sun's lower limb, having passed through a greater mass of air near sunset or sunrise, is affected more than light from the Sun's upper limb. The Sun's shape seems to change as it gets closer and closer to the horizon.

The greater air mass near sunset or sunrise also results in more scattering of blue light and greater absorption. The Sun gets redder and dimmer as it approaches the horizon, and the sky's color is consequently altered.

All of these optical effects occur under even the most pristine of skies. When we attempt to observe from an urban (or even a suburban) environment, the situation becomes more complex.

Urban Observing

Astronomical observers at sea-level sites in western Europe and eastern North America are affected by some of the most variable meteorology in the world because of the sometimes dramatic interactions between continental and maritime air masses. Fog, cloudiness, seasonal thunderstorms, and other factors all take their toll on the visibility of celestial objects.

For this reason, most of the professional observatories in the United States are located in the western states and Hawaii. However, even in these relatively pristine environments, astronomy has its problems.

The sprawling, automobile-dependent suburban culture in the Los Angeles/San Diego vicinity tends to experience impenetrable smog during the day because the intense California sunlight induces photochemical reactions in the low-level smog layer. After sunset, though, as the (solar) energy source for this chemistry decreases and vanishes, the air rapidly clears. It is no accident that some of our major astronomical observatories are located in California.

In the high desert states, the fall of night is equally dramatic, with one major difference. Because of the greatly reduced water-vapor content, or humidity, less of the solar radiation absorbed by Earth's surface during the day and reradiated as infrared is absorbed in the lower atmosphere. This reduced greenhouse effect in the arid regions results in a wide temperature swing between day

17

and night. The air temperature may be a comfortable 80 degrees Fahrenheit by day; after dusk, it rapidly approaches freezing.

During times of rapid temperature shifts, astronomical observing will be difficult because of the contraction and expansion of telescope components. After the temperature has stabilized, astronomical viewing from nonurban high desert locations is generally excellent. Because of the lower concentration of water vapor in the atmosphere, observations can be made farther into the infrared range of the electromagnetic spectrum than is possible from many other locations. However, a number of southwest desert urban areas, particularly Denver, are affected by smog.

Many major observatories are located in the mountains of Arizona and Colorado. Although astronomers often wear well-insulated and electrically heated clothing to overcome discomfort caused by the diurnal temperature swing, the future utility of these research institutes is threatened by a more insidious opponent. As the western cities spread, urban sprawl is beginning to encroach upon the domain of the astronomer. As we have seen, city lights can easily obscure a photon of light that has crossed half the universe and just fallen upon a telescope mirror. In regions where astronomical research is a major component of the local economy, "treaties" have been drawn up between scientists and bureaucrats to select the least invasive varieties of streetlights.

A number of amateur and professional astronomers have recently teamed up to combat the effects of urban light pollution. An organization devoted to countering this astronomical nuisance is The International Dark Sky Association (IDA), which is located at 3545 N. Stewart Avenue, Tucson, Arizona 85716.

In the July 1990 issue of *Sky & Telescope*, IDA members David L. Crawford and Tim B. Hunter discuss the progress of the battle against light pollution. The problem has grown so severe that our galaxy's local spiral arm, the Milky Way, is no longer visible from most urban (and many suburban) locations. The 100-inch Mount Wilson telescope, which was used early in this century by Edwin Hubble in his pioneering observational work on other galaxies, is now no longer useful in extragalactic research because of light pollution emanating from nearby Los Angeles.

Even rural sites far distant from western cities are being affected. Enhanced sky brightness, or "skyglow," due to a large urban complex is visible more than 100 miles away from that source. At a rural amateur observing station 50 miles from Tucson, one-quarter of the northeastern sky is affected by sky-glow. Even in isolated locations, unshielded night-security lights can ruin sky visibility.

In Arizona, urban sprawl has been countered somewhat by the local concentration of many of this country's largest observatories and a brave and vocal band of devoted amateurs. Comparative studies have been made of the various options available to satisfy the apparently conflicting demands for urban street-lighting and night sky visibility.

The worst streetlights are incandescent fixtures since they duplicate the wide spectral band of sunlight. Yellow incandescent "bug" lights are close runners-up for last place.

Fluorescent fixtures are somewhat better. Although a continuous (many-colored) spectrum is still present, it is dimmer than in most incandescent fixtures. Most of the lamp's energy output is in a series of spectral emission lines in the blue and yellow regions. (Just as an interstellar atom heats up by absorbing selected colors from the spectra of starlight traversing space, spectral emission lines are formed when excited atoms cool off or relax by emitting photons of specific colors.)

Mercury-vapor and halogen light fixtures are better still from the point of view of the urban astronomer. The continuous spectrum, or continuum, is dimmer, and proportionally more of the emitted light is in the bright spectral emission lines.

In high-pressure sodium lamps, the continuum is dimmer still and is limited mainly to the red and yellow regions of the spectrum. The best light fixture for the purpose of the urban astronomer is the low-pressure sodium lamp. In low-pressure sodium lamps, the continuum is essentially invisible. Almost all of the lamp's energy output is in the form of a few spectral emission lines.

As well as best satisfying the requirements of astronomers, such fixtures are also the most economical from an energy viewpoint. Tucson has been replacing its collection of 20,000 mercury-vapor lamps with more efficient street fixtures. (In fact, the use of the older lamps will be illegal after mid-1991.) Because less wattage is needed by the more efficient fixtures to satisfy the same nighttime illumination requirements, Crawford and Hunter estimate that the city will save approximately $400,000 per year. If the entire country were to follow Tucson's progressive example in replacing mercury-vapor fixtures, the energy savings might approximate $200 million per year. Extrapolating to replacement of *all* outdoor light fixtures with the most efficient ones available suggests that annual energy savings for the United States might reach an astounding $2 billion!

The type of lamp used in a streetlight is not the only factor determining its impact on astronomy or economy. One important contributor is directionality. It makes little sense, from either an astronomical or economic viewpoint, to design and install omnidirectional light fixtures. Both causes are best served by the use of shielded fixtures, which reflect lamp emissions to the level of the street where they are needed rather than to the night sky where they are not.

Urban Observing Activities

A number of actions and activities are recommended to amateur astronomers by the IDA. You might consider participating in regional and national activities of the various major environmental organizations—for example, the Audubon Society, National Geographic Society, National Wildlife Federation, and Sierra Club. Although these organizations generally deal with more direct environmental threats such as air and water pollution, some of them might get involved in the fight against skyglow. After all, as well as astronomers, various nocturnal species are adversely impacted by light pollution.

To gauge the effects of lighting in your city, you should observe the skyglow carefully from a number of locations. Try to see how much of the sky is affected and in what directions. On clear, moonless nights, you could try sketching the stars and constellation patterns visible to your unaided eye. Working with the definition of apparent visual star magnitude (see Appendix 8) and catalogs of visible bright stars, you could arrive at an estimate of limiting magnitude in your locale. You should do this at a number of sky locations, including the overhead point (or zenith) and 45 degrees altitude (midway between zenith and horizon) to the north, east, south, and west of your observing site.

Next, you might try repeating this exercise after driving a few miles out of town. In this manner, by observing progressively farther from the center of your city, you can estimate how far you must travel from your urban station to escape the effects of skyglow. You should keep in mind that light pollution will vary greatly throughout a typical city. Even if your city suffers from severe light pollution, you probably will find sites such as parks, building roofs, beaches, or lakefronts that provide suitable observatory locations.

If you decide to pursue this subject in depth, you might wish to repeat the exercise at regular time intervals. This approach will allow you to determine how astronomical viewing from your site is varying with time. If you contact the IDA, they will supply you with standardized film and exposure techniques for gauging light pollution with wide-angle photography of the night sky. ■

Streetlights and a complex regional meteorology are not the only problems facing the astronomical observer in an eastern city. He or she must also contend with the micrometeorology of an urban site.

Cities are like great heat engines. As you operate your furnace, automobile, or air conditioner, you are converting one form of energy to another. For example, a gas furnace converts chemical energy into heat. This heat is then circulated through the house using the circulation of a heated fluid—usually water. Even in the best insulated house, some heat escapes to the environment.

Because of the large urban population density (the large number of people, businesses, homes, and cars), large quantities of heat are constantly being transferred to the urban atmosphere. Because of the second law of thermodynamics, no amount of improved insulation and energy-conversion efficiency will completely eliminate this effect. In the "urban heat island," temperatures will always be a few degrees higher than in the surrounding suburban and rural communities.

The second law of thermodynamics is basically a formal codification of a technological inefficiency that is built into the structure of the universe. Whenever you convert energy from one form to another—say, stored chemical energy in your car's battery into electricity—you can never retrieve all of the initial energy in the desired form. No matter how efficient your technology, some of the stored energy *must* be converted into heat during the energy-conversion process.

Some of the heat produced in the urban environment will ultimately appear as heated air. This air, with higher temperature and lower density than the ever-present environmental air, will tend to rise. As the rising air intermingles with environmental air above an urban site, the resulting convection currents will interfere with astronomical observations. The increased air turbulence will result in greater star "twinkle." Celestial objects will seem to dance around or shimmer in the telescope eyepiece.

Because of the higher temperature, snow melts faster in the city than in surrounding rural locations. Of greater significance from an astronomical point of view, the water-vapor carrying capacity of the urban atmosphere will be greater because of the higher temperatures. Statistically speaking, urban and suburban sites will tend to be a bit cloudier than the surrounding countryside.

Also, the chemical efficiency of our internal combustion engines is less than 100 percent. Automobiles, power plants, and factories all contribute a certain amount of visual pollution. Many commentators have described the effects of these pollutants in contributing to our glorious sunrises and sunsets. Whether or not these effects have been overstated, smog certainly decreases sky transparency.

Smog has this effect because the additional particles in the atmosphere result in a higher degree of light scattering. For most smogs, particles are large enough so that the increase in scattering is wavelength (or color) independent. Some smogs, however, consist of particles of the right size and shape to preferentially scatter light of certain colors in certain directions. Brilliant cloud-color effects during urban sunrises and sunsets are thought by some scholars to be caused by increased forward scattering of violet light. Therefore, more light of selected colors from the rising or setting Sun may reach the observer's eye through certain smogs than might be seen in the absence of smog.

It would be a mistake to believe that any of these sky effects, natural or artificial, are uniform over a region as large as a major city. To celebrate a summer 1989 lunar eclipse visible from New York City, concurrent observing sessions were scheduled in Manhattan's Central Park, Flushing Meadow Park in Queens, and Gateway National Park in Brooklyn. Much to the disappointment of many would-be eclipse viewers, two of the three sites (all of which are separated by a few miles) were completely socked in by clouds and rain. At Gateway, however, the clouds parted and the Moon was briefly visible shortly after totality. Some of the regional variation in clouds and rain in a large city might be due to variations in urban temperature; most of it is probably due to intrinsic characteristics of the air masses responsible for the clouds and rain.

Observing sites in city parks, near the shore, or in similarly isolated locations are blessed with slightly dimmer skies than are other urban locations. However, no urban sky will ever approach the glory of the night sky in a more isolated location.

Seasonal variations are another consideration. In the summer, nighttime sky observing from urban locations is difficult because of the long days and short nights. Most people are less than ready to venture to an isolated urban viewing site after 9 or 10 P.M.

During the winter, colder sky temperatures result in lower levels of atmospheric moisture. Although the skies are clearer and the nights longer, few souls are hardy enough to brave subfreezing evening temperatures in northern cities. At this time of year, urban astronomers in warm locations such as Miami, Los Angeles, and Dallas have a distinct advantage over their snowbound northern colleagues!

One way around some of these difficulties is a terrace or rooftop observing location. Many roofs are above the level of the streetlights and have ready access to warm building interiors. Some, but not all, roofs are stable enough to maintain the weight of a telescope tripod and some intrepid observers. You should, of course, check the condition of the roof before scheduling your observing session there. A roof collapse would be dangerous, not to mention embarrassing and expensive! Tar roofs in particular should not be walked upon.

If you observe from a location equipped with shielded and high-efficiency streetlamps, the advantages of an observing station on even a low roof will be immediately apparent. Most of the light emitted from the lamps is at or near street level; little of it will "leak" more than one story above the ground.

Rooftop Observing Checklist

In considering an observing session from an urban rooftop location, there are a number of factors that you should keep in mind. These include:

1. *Roof access.* If you are observing with the naked eye or binoculars, it does not matter exactly how you get to your roof. However, ladder access is a definite limitation if you are lugging even a small telescope up with you.

2. *Can the roof support the weight of your equipment?* Most, if not all, roofs are constructed of material that can easily support a human being. Even though a telescope on a tripod is usually of lesser weight than a small person, this does not mean that your roof can support the telescope. The weight per unit tripod area is a factor that might cause your instrument to begin slipping into the roof material. To reduce the possibility of expensive roof repairs, you should check with your building's superintendent or examine roof plans on file with the appropriate municipal agency.

3. *Is the roof fenced?* For your protection and comfort, it would be better not to observe from an unfenced roof. It is very easy to be carried away by the beauties of the objects you are observing—and it is a long way down!

4. *And what of the neighbors?* Many people living in high-rises become somewhat jealous of their privacy when they realize that the urban astronomer on the building roof across from them could easily look in their windows with a telescope. To preserve neighborhood harmony, it may be a good idea to discuss your rooftop astronomical observatory with people in your line of sight before you actually observe. Even better, invite them along! ■

Usually, the best seasons for evening sky observing sessions in northern cities are spring and autumn. Temperatures are moderate and the skies darken sufficiently by 6 or 7 P.M. so that some sky objects are visible. On a clear night, the Moon, naked-eye planets, bright stars, and some familiar constellations can all be observed.

One paradox of locating an observing site within a large urban area is the natural reluctance of most law-abiding citizens to venture out on parkland at night. The fear of the mugger, rapist, or drug pusher is sometimes overwhelming.

A partial solution to this problem is to form alliances with the uniformed services. It is a very good idea to obtain a permit for your activities in the park. This will let park authorities know that you are there. Sometimes, members of the uniformed park services will escort you to and from your observing site and check in on you periodically during your observing session.

Park Observing Checklist

In beginning to plan observing sessions within a municipal park, there are a few factors that you should consider. These include:

1. *Accessibility of observing location.* Even though a site deep in the park may be darker, it is farther away from "civilization." Late at night, urban sky observers laden with expensive telescopes will find a remote site rather scary.

2. *Local topographic variations.* You should visit your proposed site in the daytime and, if possible, consult topographic maps available from your municipal authorities. If your site is in a local depression, the view of the sky may be restricted. A flat or elevated site is superior. You should also perform a site visit to check for trees and other vegetation that might obscure your view of portions of the sky near the horizon.

3. *Availability of public facilities.* In planning a long evening in the park, you should check that clean restrooms are available.

4. *Is a permit required?* You should check with your municipal park service to learn whether a permit is required for night-time park use. If the authorities are aware of your presence, park police may check on your safety during the evening. Their attention can be quite reassuring!

5. *Dress warmly.* After nightfall, the temperature in the urban parkland often drops dramatically. To ensure comfort and preserve health, it pays to wear an extra layer or two of clothing. ■

Perhaps the nicest thing about astronomy is its timeless nature, at least from the human viewpoint. A great deal of knowledge and enjoyment can result from a naked-eye observing session even when we leave our expensive gadgets at home. The joys of naked-eye astronomy are partially explored in the next chapter.

CHAPTER 2

Patterns in the Sky

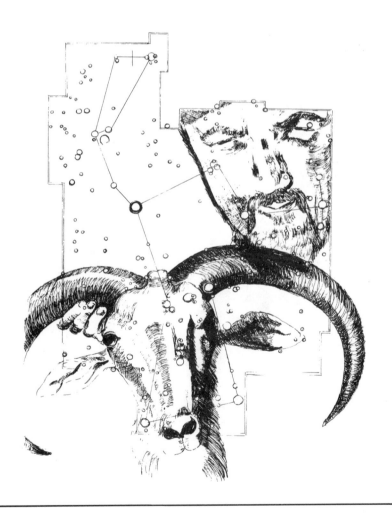

Never did I fail
Of an answer back
To the zodiac
When in heartless chorus
Aries and Taurus,
Gemini and Cancer
Mocked me for an answer.
　　　—Robert Frost, *Kitty Hawk* (1962)

From the murky setting of the modern city, fewer stars are visible than could be seen by the ancients. We have seen that tall buildings obscure some stars, smog scatters light from others, and skyglow can render the sky brighter than many stars visible from a rural site.

Still, many of the brighter stars are often visible from an urban viewing site. Some of the sky patterns called *constellations* can also be recognized, especially if you follow the tips outlined in this book.

Very ancient people determined the shapes of the original constellations. Familiar animals, mythological figures, and musical instruments were all pictured in the sky by these ancients probably because these items were easy to remember.

The constellations served as benchmarks for motions of the Moon, Sun, and planets. As such, they became important in calendar studies, navigation, and the art of astrology.

A long-term wobble of Earth, known as *precession,* causes the direction of Earth's axis to slowly change. Because of this precessional motion, the location of the Celestial North Pole (the projection of Earth's north pole on the sky) varies over a 26,000-year period. Polaris (the tail star in Ursa Minor, the Little Dipper or Little Bear) has not always been the north star. Today, the Celestial North Pole is within 1/2 a degree of Polaris. (You can readily observe precession by using a toy gyroscope or spinning top. If you start the toy spinning so that its axis is not perfectly vertical, you will notice that the spin-axis does not always point in the same direction. Instead, it rotates through a cone, or precesses. The spinning Earth repeats the same process on a larger and slower scale.)

Precessional changes also alter, over a period of thousands of years, the constellation that the Sun is in during a given month. Stars move across the heavens with their own slow (from our point of view) proper motions. Over periods of thousands of years, the shapes of the recognizable constellations are altered.

Different epochs in history have therefore seen different pole stars and different constellations. We may expect that many of those sky patterns now recognized by astronomers will similarly become obsolete in future centuries.

No attempt is made here to discuss all of the 89 currently recognized constellations. We will focus only on those patterns that are easy to recognize in the gloomy skies of a mid-latitude city in the Northern Hemisphere.

For convenience, constellations are broken up into several classes. Circumpolar constellations, which include Ursa Major (the Big Dipper), Ursa Minor, Draco, Cepheus, and Cassiopeia, are always above the horizon because of their proximity to the pole star. Seasonal constellations, which are farther away from the north pole of the celestial sphere, are visible in the night sky only at certain times of year. Those seasonal constellations that are close to the path of the planets and the Sun—the ecliptic—constitute the 12 constellations of the zodiac. These stellar patterns—Aries, Taurus, Gemini, Cancer, Leo, Virgo, Libra, Scorpio, Sagittarius, Capricorn, Aquarius, and Pisces—have been of significance to astrologers for at least 3,000 years.

Appendix 6 provides seasonal star charts showing the positions of the zodiacal constellations. During the winter, Leo, Gemini, Taurus, Aries, and Pisces are visible in the evening sky. On spring evenings, the naked-eye observer can locate the positions of Libra, Virgo, Leo, Cancer, Gemini, and Taurus. Zodiacal constellations in the summer evening skies include Capricorn, Sagittarius, Scorpio, Libra, and Virgo. Six zodiacal constellations can be viewed on autumn evenings. These are Taurus, Aries, Pisces, Aquarius, Capricorn, and Sagittarius.

The star charts in Appendix 6 also give some pointers for the seasonal observation of the circumpolar constellations. The Big Dipper (Ursa Major) is always the easiest constellation to recognize; the Little Dipper (Ursa Minor) may not be easy to find if your observing site suffers from too much skyglow. Cepheus usually resembles an upside-down house, and Cassiopeia is like the letter *W* or (depending upon the season) an inverted *W*, or *M*.

All of the circumpolar constellations can be viewed from a mid-latitude northern city such as Los Angeles or New York, although the urban haze will obscure some of them at certain times of year. Among the zodiacal 12, Gemini, Taurus, Leo, and Virgo are the easiest to locate and observe. Important nonzodiacal seasonal constellations that are easy to locate (after a little practice) include Lyra, Cygnus, Aquila, Andromeda, Auriga, Canis Major and Canis Minor (the Big and Little Dogs), and Boötes (the Herdsman).

Because the patterns of many of the constellations may be difficult to observe in bright urban skies, other tools may be used to locate the position of these sky patterns. Gemini can be recognized by its two bright stars, Castor and Pollux. Taurus and Virgo can be found by locating their brightest stars, Aldebaran and Spica, respectively. Leo contains the bright star Regulus. A portion of this constellation resembles a sickle. If you can locate the brightest stars in the summer sky, Vega, Altair, and Deneb, then you have also found the constellations Lyra, Aquila, and Cygnus.

Also in the clear late summer or autumn sky, you can view the Great Nebula M31 in Andromeda with the naked eye and thereby locate this constellation. In November at 9 P.M., Andromeda is almost directly overhead.

The brightest star in the night sky, Sirius, is in Canis Major (the Big Dog). Another bright star, Procyon, is in Canis Minor. Bright red Arcturus, which can be found by following the "arc" of the stars in the handle of the Big Dipper, is the brightest star in Boötes. The fourth brightest star in the sky is near the zenith on winter evenings. This is Capella in the constellation Auriga.

What follows is an attempt to give novice sky observers some hints and signposts for finding their way around the evening sky.

The mythology of the constellations is mostly left behind here. Instead, these sky patterns are treated as fortuitous random groupings of stars that just happen to be easy to recognize. For best results, you should refer to the seasonal evening sky maps and the table of bright stars that are included in Appendices 6 and 9.

A Novice Views the Sky

To identify the constellations or to reacquaint themselves with the skies after a hiatus between viewing sessions, novice observers may wish to follow the strategy outlined here.

The first step is to locate the geographical north. In gloomy urban skies, Polaris may not always be easily visible. It pays to carry a compass. On most evenings, Ursa Major will be quite apparent if you look toward the north. In a recent consideration of constellation lore, George Lovi points out that many people have seen this grouping as a plough or a wagon. One indication of the very ancient connection of American Indian and Asian cultures is the interpretation of this grouping as a bear in both traditions. The big dipper representation apparently dates to nineteenth-century America.

Once you have found Ursa Major, it is easy to locate Polaris by using the two end stars in the dipper's cup as pointers. Polaris is the tail star in Ursa Minor.

In between the two dippers snakes sinuous Draco (the Dragon). This mythological beast was associated in ancient Greek mythology with the guardian of the golden apples of the garden of Hesperides and was dispatched by the hero Hercules. To the Egyptians, Draco represented a crocodile or hippopotamus. When pharonic Egypt was in its prime, Thuban (Alpha Draconis, the brightest star in Draco) was the north star.

During the winter and spring, the constellation Orion (the Hunter) is particularly easy to find, perhaps because of the three almost perfectly aligned stars in Orion's belt. One of two very bright stars in Orion is the red giant Betelgeuse (Alpha Orionis) on the hunter's left shoulder (from our point of view). Betelgeuse, a variable red giant star, is the ninth brightest star in the sky. Rigel

(Beta Orionis) is a blue supergiant. (For more information on the significance of stellar colors and sizes, consult Chapter 6 and Appendix 7, which deals with stellar evolution and the Hertzsprung–Russell diagram.) Rigel, which is slightly brighter than Betelgeuse, is located (also from our point of view) on the hunter's right foot. Hanging down from his belt are the stars constituting Orion's sword. Just below these, and a beautiful sight in binoculars or a small telescope, is the Great Nebula M42, a stellar nursery. Although Orion is a winter constellation now, precession will cause it to be a summer constellation in about 13,000 years.

Just west of Orion is Taurus (the Bull). This constellation contains the bright red giant Aldebaran as well as two galactic star clusters, the Pleiades and Hyades. In Greek mythology, Taurus was the creature (actually Zeus in disguise) who carried off Europa. In many renditions of the night sky, Taurus is apparently threatening Orion, who is portrayed as protecting himself with his upraised shield.

Slightly west and north of Taurus is Auriga (the Charioteer). Brilliant yellow Capella, the brightest star in Auriga, is actually a pair of gravitationally linked, or binary, stars. (For more information on binary stars, consult Chapter 6.) In the urban winter sky or on a planetarium dome, the constellation Auriga may seem to look more like a crudely drawn house than a charioteer.

In the spring, Gemini (the Twins, Castor and Pollux) is visible to the east of Orion. The Romans identified the twins with Romulus and Remus, the legendary founders of Rome. Canis Major (the Big Dog) can be picked out in the murky skies near the western horizon by the blue-white glare of Sirius, the brightest star in the sky. Sirius, incidentally, is one of the closest stellar neighbors to our Sun.

During spring evenings, Leo (the Lion) is near the zenith. Leo appears to be stalking the twins and is most easily identified by the five stars resembling a sickle.

On warm summer nights, Aquila (the Eagle) can usually be located by its birdlike shape and Cygnus (the Swan) by the prominent Northern Cross. The third bright member of "the Summer Triangle" is Vega, the brightest star in Lyra (the Harp). A blue-white dwarf considerably hotter than our Sun, Vega is the fifth brightest star in the sky. (Once again, you can learn about the significance of stellar colors, temperatures, and sizes by consulting Chapter 6 and Appendix 7.)

At 10 P.M. in July, brilliant Vega is quite close to the zenith. Long used as a calibration star in astronomical photoelectric photometry, Vega is now suspected to be accompanied by a brand-new solar system. (Astronomical photoelectric photometry is the quantitative measure of starlight intensity, in which starlight is converted into an electrical signal. More details regarding this subject are presented in Appendix 13.)

The patterns in the evening sky can be endlessly described. Some have written about the constellations in encyclopedic detail. What may be of greater use here is an outline of some constellation-gazing activities. To get the most out of your evening sky-watches, you might first concentrate upon recognizing the easy patterns such as Ursa Major, Orion, Cassiopeia, and Cepheus. Then, you might try to find some of the others by locating the positions of the bright stars listed in Appendix 9. All of these are readily visible from moderately light-free urban locations on a clear night during the appropriate season(s). If there are naked-eye planets in the skies, the tabulated data presented in Appendix 1 can be used to pinpoint these within the zodiacal constellations until the year 2001.

If you desire to supplement or replace the seasonal star charts presented in Appendix 6, you could purchase an inexpensive star finder at your local planetarium. The resources section of the book lists other sources for charts of the night sky.

Autumn Sky Constellation Activities

In the autumn sky, Ursa Major is often lost in the murky light of the urban horizon, although it is still above the horizon. Draco and Ursa Minor are higher in the sky and are more likely to be visible on a moderately clear night. Lyra, which can be located by its brightest star, Vega, is west of the zenith (the overhead point).

Cygnus (the Swan), which does seem somewhat birdlike, is closer to the zenith than is Lyra. Aquila is at about the same altitude above the horizon as is Lyra, but it is farther south. Cassiopeia, (usually identified as the letter *M* or *W*) is high in the sky.

More than halfway above the eastern horizon is Andromeda (the Chained Woman). Although you may never be fortunate enough to locate Andromeda's chains, on a clear autumn evening the Great Spiral Nebula in Andromeda is visible to the naked eye as a cloudlike structure. The brightest star in Andromeda, Alpheratz, and three neighboring bright stars in Pegasus form the Great Square.

Because Ursa Major (the Big Dipper) will probably be invisible in the skyglow near the urban horizon, you may initially require a compass to orient yourself with the constellations. After you have found geographic north, look in that direction. In early autumn, Ursa Minor (the Little Dipper) and the North Star, Polaris, should be visible on clear evenings about halfway up from the northern horizon. South of Polaris in the early autumn evening sky is Cepheus. The tip of the Cepheus "house" points north. Just east of Cepheus is Cassiopeia. At this time of year, the central prong of the *W* points west.

Now look directly overhead. The bright star is Deneb. It is in the tip of the birdlike Cygnus. If you march east from Deneb, about halfway toward the horizon, you will come upon the Great Square, formed by the brightest stars in Andromeda and Pegasus.

Early autumn constellation-hunts from urban viewing sites are gratifying. Temperatures are generally comfortable, although sweaters or light jackets are usually necessary in northern cities. The skies tend to be clear, and the Sun sets at a reasonably early hour. ∎

Winter Sky Constellation Activities

Winter evenings tend to be clearer, as well as colder, than those of the other seasons. If the hardy sky observer is able to put up with the lower temperatures, he or she will be amply rewarded by a magnificent choice of sky objects.

Ursa Major and Draco are both low near the western horizon. Because of the clearer winter skies, these may be readily observable from a moderately light-free location. Cassiopeia, Auriga, Gemini, Orion, and Taurus are all high in the sky. Andromeda is about halfway between the western horizon and the zenith, and the Pleiades cluster is near the zenith.

Canis Minor and Canis Major are low in the eastern sky. The brightest star in Canis Major, Sirius, (also the brightest star in the heavens), is spectacular in the winter evening skies.

If you are hearty enough to observe during a late-January evening, look first toward the northern horizon. You should be able to make out the two "pointer stars" of the Big Dipper, about one-quarter of the way up from the horizon. These two stars are the ones farthest from the handle. If you follow them from east to west, you will soon come to Polaris, the North Star.

During the winter, Cassiopeia is high in the northwestern sky. The central prong of the *W* points north. Cepheus is almost due west of Polaris. The top of the "house" is pointing east.

Now look toward the overhead point (or zenith). Just east of the zenith is Capella, the brightest star in Auriga. About halfway between the zenith and the eastern horizon are Castor and Pollux, which form Gemini (the Twins). Closer still to the eastern horizon is Procyon, the brightest star in Canis Minor.

A bit southeast of the zenith is Aldebaran, the bright red star in Taurus. If you draw an imaginary line between Taurus and the western horizon, you will first come to the Hyades cluster and then to the easily visible cluster, the Pleiades.

About one-third of the distance between the eastern horizon and the zenith is Sirius (the brightest star in the sky) in Canis Major. Between Sirius and Taurus is Orion, one of the most distinctive constellations in the sky.

During winter evenings, the eastern part of the sky is much more interesting than the western portion. The Great Square of Andromeda and Pegasus, however, is visible about one-third of the way between the western horizon and the zenith. ∎

Spring Sky Constellation Activities

During the spring, as the weather warms and the days lengthen, Cassiopeia and Cepheus are close to the northern horizon. Ursa Major, Ursa Minor, and Draco are all higher in the northern sky and are consequently easier to observe.

Leo is near the zenith; Orion and Taurus are setting in the west. Virgo and Boötes are about one-third of the distance to the zenith above the eastern horizon. Canis Major, Canis Minor, and Gemini are about the same distance above the western horizon. Spring observing sessions are generally a great deal of fun because of the warming temperatures and the usually clear skies.

If you decide to celebrate the vernal equinox by observing constellations during an early-April evening, no compass will be necessary to find the North Star. The Big Dipper is high in the sky and a bit northeast of the zenith. You can easily follow the pointer stars of the Big Dipper toward the northwest until you reach Polaris.

Now look at the arc formed by the three stars in the Big Dipper's handle. If you follow this curve away from the dipper's cup, you will come to the bright star Arcturus in the constellation Boötes. Arcturus is due east of the Big Dipper at this time. Much closer to the eastern horizon and along the same arc is Spica in Virgo. This bright, blue-green star may be lost in the urban skyglow of the eastern horizon.

A bit southeast of the zenith is the sickle of Leo and the bright star Regulus. West of the zenith, you will easily locate Gemini (the Twins, Castor and Pollux). To the south of Gemini is Procyon, the bright star in Canis Minor. Farther west from Procyon is Sirius, the brightest star in the sky.

The distinctive pattern of Orion is low in the western sky but should still be visible on a moderately clear evening. A bit north of Orion is Taurus. Although the Pleiades and Hyades clusters in Taurus may be difficult to find from an urban observing site on an early-April evening, Aldebaran (the brightest star in this constellation) should be visible low in the west. About midway between the zenith and the western horizon, you will easily spot another bright star. This is Capella in the constellation Auriga. ■

Summer Sky Constellation Activities

Although outdoor temperatures in the summer are usually comfortable, summer observing sessions are less satisfying from observing sites located in relatively humid cities. Cloudiness, thunderstorms, and haze often conspire against the urban astronomer hoping to observe under comfortable conditions.

On the rare clear summer night, Ursa Major, Ursa Minor, and Draco are all a good distance above the northern horizon. Cassiopeia and Cepheus, however, are closer to the northern horizon and may be more difficult to observe.

If you follow the arc of the handle of the Big Dipper, you will readily spot Arcturus, the bright red star in the constellation Boötes. Aquila, Cygnus, and Lyra are all sufficiently high in the eastern sky to be easily seen. Deneb, the brightest star in Cygnus; Altair, the chief luminary in Aquila; and Vega, the brilliant star in Lyra constitute the Summer Triangle. Cygnus is also distinguishable as the Northern Cross. During summer evenings, Virgo and Leo are fairly low in the west and therefore may be difficult to spot.

During mid-July at 9:30 P.M., the intrepid sky observer (coated with insect repellent) will observe the Big Dipper in the northwest. Following the dipper's pointer stars to the east, you will soon locate Polaris. If you follow the arc of the dipper's handle star to the south, Arcturus in Boötes will be easily found.

High in the eastern sky is the Summer Triangle. Vega is closest to the zenith, and Altair is halfway between the zenith and the eastern horizon. Deneb is northeast of Vega.

As previously mentioned, summer observing from urban sites can be disappointing. On a very clear night, you may catch a glimpse of the "house" of Cepheus, about one-third of the way up from the northeastern horizon. The top of the house points northwest.

Closer to the northern horizon and usually invisible in the urban summer sky is Cassiopeia. If you face north, this constellation will look like the letter *M*.

Two other bright stars are also in the summer evening sky, but they may be too low to be easily observable from an urban site. These are Spica in Virgo, which is setting in the west, and Antares in Scorpio, which is low in the south. ■

CHAPTER 3

Astronomer's Eyes

He, who through vast immensity can pierce,
See worlds on worlds compose one universe,
Observe how system into system runs,
What other planets circle other suns,
What varied Being peoples every star,
May tell why Heaven has made us as we are.
—Alexander Pope, *An Essay on Man, Epistle I*
(1733–1734)

This chapter deals with the basic tools that the urban astronomer uses to gather information about the heavens. All optical devices used, whether they are telescopes or binoculars, are nothing more than specialized analogs of the human eye, which is still the best general-purpose light detector in existence.

In considering the details of the specific optical devices used to collect starlight, a few basic concepts should first be understood. One term that is often used is *aperture,* which refers to the physical size of the main optical element (lens or mirror) of the instrument under consideration.

In astronomical photoelectric photometry, starlight is often converted into electrical current, which is measured in amperes. If you are using a *linear optical detector,* you will notice a direct relationship between the observed light intensity and the electrical current. This means that if you shift to a light source 10 times (10X) as intense, the resulting electrical current will go up by a corresponding factor of 10. Because the human eye has a variable aperture, it is a nonlinear detector.

The human eye, and that of other vertebrates, has several basic components. Basically, a focusing lens is suspended in a fluid in front of the retina, which is the sensory layer. Light enters the eye through a central opening, the pupil. The size of the pupil is controlled by the iris, a pigmented layer that is regulated by muscles to open or close in response to higher or lower illumination levels. The lower the light level, the wider the opening.

Signals from the retina are transmitted to the brain by the optic nerve. The rods and cones on the retina are the basic color sensors of the human eye. Astronomers have long recognized that it is important at night to maintain the eye's "dark adaptation." This requirement often conflicts with the necessity of some nonstellar illumination to read a star chart, change an eyepiece, or perform some other duty. One commonly practiced solution is to use only red tinted lights during an observing session since this color is less deleterious to dark adaptation than other colors.

The fact that the iris can regulate pupil size in response to incident illumination level (the amount of light striking the eye) allows us to see both during the day and night and contributes to the eye's function as a nonlinear detector. Hipparchus, one of the great astronomers of antiquity, created a catalog of about 850 stars during the second century of the pre-Christian era. He divided the stars up into six magnitude categories, with magnitude 1 as the brightest visible to the eye and magnitude 6 as the dimmest visible. (Modern astronomers call Hipparchus's list a tabulation of *visual apparent magnitudes* to differentiate from the *absolute magnitude* system, which corrects for the different distances to the stars.) Hipparchus reasoned that a magnitude 3 star is twice as bright as a magnitude 4 star; a magnitude 1 star is twice as bright as a magnitude 2 star; and so on.

When a modern astronomer checks Hipparchus's tabulation with a linear optical detector such as the photoelectric cell, he or she finds that magnitude 1 stars are *not* twice as bright as magnitude 2 stars but are in actuality about 2.5 times as bright. (If the eye were a linear detector, the ratio would be 2 times.) More information on magnitude systems is presented in Appendix 8.

Every astronomer, whether amateur or professional, is faced with the same problems—namely, how to make very distant objects appear closer, how to resolve surface details on a distant world, and how to render the invisible visible.

Perhaps as early as the thirteenth century, lens makers had discovered that placing one lens in front of another could make a distant object appear larger, or magnified. In the first decade of the seventeenth century, the Italian scientist Galileo Galilei applied this principle to construct the first known astronomical telescope.

Galileo's early telescope was the first refractor, an instrument that operates by the bending of light (Figure 3–1). Light from a distant object (a planet, star, or distant cloud) falls upon a large lens called the *objective*. All of the light rays are bent to converge at the same point, called the *focus*, in the ideal refractor. A second smaller lens, called the *eyepiece*, collects the light rays after they have passed through the focus and directs them to the observer's eye.

In addition to his many other accomplishments in the development of physics and higher mathematics, Sir Isaac Newton demonstrated how to replace the objective lens of Galileo's telescope with two mirrors, one curved and one plane (Figure 3–2). The curved *primary* mirror, which is larger than the flat mirror, gathers the light and directs it to the flat *secondary*. This smaller mirror reflects the light into the eyepiece. Like the refractor, the Newtonian reflector requires a long tube. Although the first successful reflector was constructed by Newton in 1668, James Gregory had actually conceived the idea five years earlier.

For centuries, astronomical reflectors and refractors were in close competition. Although lenses suffered from more serious ab-

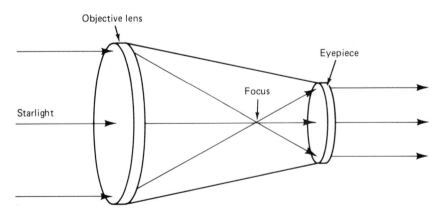

Figure 3–1   Galileo's refracting telescope

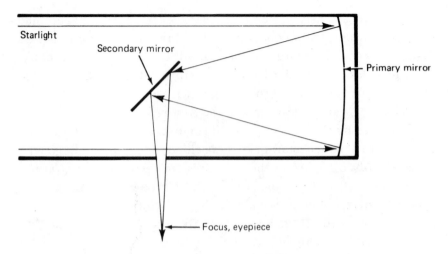

Figure 3–2 Newtonian reflecting telescope

errations, whereby light rays entering the objective at different locations or rays of different colors had different focal points, corrective mechanisms existed. Also, opticians had more experience with refracting lenses; these devices were consequently less expensive than reflectors of like size.

The great age of the refractor culminated in the 10- to 40-inch aperture instruments of Alvin Clark, which are still in use after about a century in some major observatories such as Yerkes, Van Vleck, and Allegheny. Since the turn of the twentieth century, the construction of astronomical refractors has greatly declined.

The major reason for the current ascendancy of the reflector is the success of modern opticians in replacing the plane secondary mirror of the Newtonian reflector with a curved mirror. In modern reflectors, such as the Cassegrain, the combination of curved primary and secondary mirrors is used to fold the optical path (Figure 3–3). Reflectors can therefore be more compact than corresponding refractors. Because the eyepiece of a Cassegrain can be located at the back of the tube rather than at the side as in the case of a Newtonian reflector, observers at the Cassegrain focus need not be accomplished gymnasts!

Modern Cassegrain primary mirrors still suffer from some aberrations, which tend to limit their fields of view. An Estonian op-

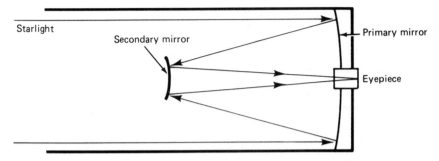

Figure 3–3 Cassegrain reflector

tician named Bernhard Schmidt solved this problem by combining attributes of the reflector and the refractor. In a Schmidt–Cassegrain telescope, a correcting lens of variable thickness is placed at the telescope tube's opening (Figure 3–4).

Astronomical telescopes invert the image and are therefore somewhat inconvenient for terrestrial use. Binoculars and similar terrestrial instruments contain internal prisms to "reinvert" the image. Another advantage of binoculars is that, unlike telescopes, they can be used by both eyes simultaneously.

In selecting an observing instrument, it is essential to take stock of the local sky conditions, economic realities, and other factors, as well as the present-day availability of excellent large-aperture optical systems. While the giant of Mount Palomar works fine in its near-pristine environment, it would certainly not see as far if moved to a station atop the World Trade Center!

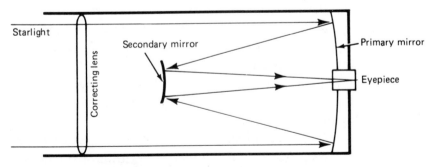

Figure 3–4 Schmidt-Cassegrain telescope

In comparing optical instruments, an astronomer looks at four basic characteristics. First, *magnification,* the apparent enlargement of a distant object, is considered. Anyone who has observed a bird sitting upon a branch of a distant tree through a pair of binoculars has experienced image magnification. A magnification of 50X increases the apparent size of the observed object by 50 times. For example, if you are observing a distant chimney consisting of 50 vertical rows of bricks, under a 50X magnification each brick will appear as tall in the telescope eyepiece as the entire chimney does to the unaided eye.

The *field of view* (often abbreviated as F.O.V.) is also a significant factor. A greatly magnified image of a distant sky object is of little value if the field of view, the angular portion of the sky visible at any one time in the eyepiece, is so small that even an experienced observer cannot locate the object in the telescope's eyepiece. In many cases, a high-magnification eyepiece is one with a correspondingly low field of view. The experienced sky observer will often center the target with a low-magnification eyepiece and then transfer to higher magnification.

It is necessary to find a viable compromise between magnification and F.O.V. In the turbulent skies of the urban environment, you will find that very high magnification and low F.O.V. are difficult to work with. A magnification much in excess of 130X is rarely useful. For most urban applications, magnifications in the 35X–65X range are quite sufficient. Only under very rare urban observing conditions are magnifications greater than 40X per inch of telescope aperture useful.

Of equal importance is the *resolving power.* The resolving power is the ability of the telescope to supply images of fine details such as the wings on a distant bird or the mountain in a lunar crater. Resolving power depends not so much upon the system's magnification as upon the size of the entrance aperture. Assuming equal optical quality and good sky conditions, a 4-inch diameter telescope will be able to resolve craters on the moon twice as small as a 2-inch diameter telescope.

Finally, the astronomer must consider the *light-gathering power* of the telescope. A useful model is to think of the optical system as a "photon bucket." The photon is the smallest discrete quantity of light. Think of the photons as water drops in a rainstorm and the telescope as a bucket open to the storm. The number of raindrops gathered will depend upon the area of the bucket. A 4-inch diameter telescope will therefore collect 4 times as much light as a corresponding 2-inch diameter telescope. The basic effect of increased light-gathering power is to make dim objects seem brighter at the telescope's focus.

All astronomers would like to maximize field of view, magnification, resolution, and light-gathering power. For urban astronomers, instrument portability is also significant. Many urban astronomers consider apertures from 3 to 8 inches to be the best.

Many commercially available telescopes are equipped with electrical clock drives. With such a device, a properly aligned telescope can compensate for Earth's motion. Once a sky object is centered in the field of view, it will remain all night, with only minor adjustments. A modern clock drive need not be terribly expensive. If you purchase one as an accessory with your telescope, the cost of the instrument will not increase by more than $100 or so. Although not essential to urban sky viewing, the clock drive is convenient if you plan to observe one sky object for more than a few minutes or to try your hand at astrophotography.

Another useful attachment on many commercially available telescopes is the finder scope. If aligned with the main optics (or bore-sighted), this low-magnification, high field-of-view tool can be used to find and center a star's image in the main scope.

If you intend to measure angular separations or sizes of celestial objects, a very useful accessory for your telescope is a reticle eyepiece. Such an eyepiece projects an illuminated cross-hair, grid, or circular pattern over the celestial view so that relative sizes and positions can be quantitatively measured.

If you scan the pages of *Sky & Telescope* and *Astronomy* magazines, you will be impressed and appalled by the sheer quantity of kinds of telescopes available. There are refractors in a very wide price range, Newtonian reflectors, wide-field Newtonians, Cassegrains, and Schmidt–Cassegrains. You can spend $100 on a telescope—or $100,000.

For the investment of a far more trifling amount of money, you can obtain a small refracting telescope capable of duplicating the original observations of Galileo Galilei. This might be a nice, risk-free means of getting into telescopic astronomy.

The Harvard-Smithsonian Center for Astrophysics, in Cambridge, Massachusetts, is conducting Project STAR (Science Teaching through its Astronomical Roots). In the April 1990 issue of *Sky & Telescope*, Alan MacRobert describes a very inexpensive but illuminating astronomy activity developed by STAR.

According to his article, for a mere $5, you can obtain the lenses to reconstruct a simple refracting telescope with the same performance as the one utilized by Galileo Galilei to first probe the heavens. With such a primitive and simple instrument, the original telescopic observations of the Moon (Figure 3–5) and the moons of Jupiter can be duplicated. Although Saturn's rings will not be resolved through such an instrument, the observer will readily learn why early observers mistook Saturn for a triple planet (Figure 3–6).

At least for most astronomers, the novelty of repeating early observations will soon wear off. More modern instruments will soon command your attention.

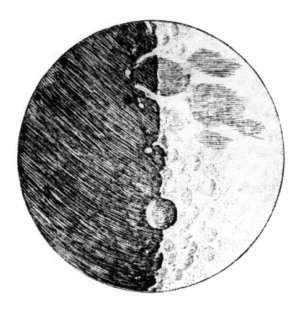

Figure 3–5 One of Galileo's drawings of the Moon (From A. Berry, *A Short History of Astronomy*. Courtesy Dover Publications, Inc.)

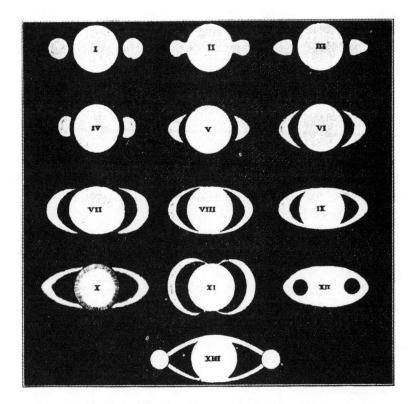

Figure 3-6 Early telescope drawings of Saturn (From A. Berry, *A Short History of Astronomy*. Courtesy Dover Publications, Inc.)

For evening observing sessions far from home, you will require instruments that are durable, portable, and equipped with excellent optics. Wide-field Newtonians designed for field use are especially effective. These can be purchased for a few hundred dollars.

If you have a bit more money and an outdoor source of electricity near your viewing location, a Schmidt–Cassegrain telescope with an aperture of 4 inches might be a good choice. This type of telescope is usually equipped with an electrically powered clock drive, which allows the telescope to follow an object centered in the F.O.V. so that constant readjustment is not required.

For solar viewing, both 4-inch and 8-inch aperture Schmidt–Cassegrains equipped with appropriate filters may be used (see

Chapter 7). Although the image is more detailed in the larger instrument, sunspots are clearly visible through the eyepiece of the properly filtered smaller telescope. One person can easily handle the 4-inch telescope. A crew of two or three is required to assemble, carry, and disassemble a typical 8-inch Schmidt–Cassegrain at a field location.

Refractors are generally more expensive than reflectors of equal aperture. If you plan on getting involved with astrophotography from a dark site, a 3- or 4-inch aperture refractor equipped with a clock drive might be the ideal instrument for you.

Binoculars also have a significant role in urban sky observing. A low magnification (5X–8X) brings out some lunar detail and renders the large satellites of Jupiter (Callisto, Europa, Ganymede, and Io) clearly visible (see Chapter 5). Binoculars can also resolve the disks of Venus and Mars. Under good urban viewing conditions, you should be able to spot Saturn's rings and view the phases of Venus through your binoculars. Many double stars are also clearly visible in low-power binoculars, as are star colors. Some deep-sky objects, notably the Great Nebula in the constellation Orion (see Chapter 6), are colorful through binoculars.

In a typical evening observing session, you might want to bring along a 4-inch aperture wide-field Newtonian telescope, a pair of binoculars, a star map, and compass. Reserve the telescope at first for sighting upon the Moon and whatever planets are visible. As the evening wears on, you will begin to appreciate the advantage of the binoculars' portability.

Colorful stars, like the blue giant Rigel and the red giant Betelgeuse, both of which are in the constellation Orion, seem more spectacular through telescopes. Prominent double stars, such as Alcor and Mizar, both of which are in the handle of the Big Dipper, stand out nicely in binoculars and small telescopes.

Some deep-sky objects are observable with small-aperture equipment in an urban setting. The spiral galaxy M31 in Andromeda and the Orion nebula are particularly striking. The latter object, a star nursery in which new stars are condensing from interstellar dust and gas, stands out as a brilliant greenish blue cloud, illuminated by the infant stars within it. The Andromeda Galaxy is best viewed during the late summer or autumn; Orion is clearly visible on clear winter evenings. (Refer to Chapter 6 and Appendix 6 for more information.)

No matter what optical detector astronomers use, it is important for them to be able to find their way around the sky. This is accomplished using various coordinate systems. Most of these make the mathematical assumption that the Sun, Moon, stars, and planets are on a series of transparent spheres centered on Earth, much like the now-discredited Ptolemaic view of the Solar System.

The most basic of the sky observer's coordinate systems is the *altitude–azimuth system* (often abbreviated as alt–az). In the alt–az system, the vertical angular distance of a celestial object above or below the horizon is the altitude. Its angular distance (eastward) from compass north is its azimuth. A star directly overhead is at the *zenith*, with an altitude of 90 degrees. Similarly, the point on the mythical celestial sphere that is directly below your feet is the *nadir* and has an altitude of −90 degrees. The local meridian is a north–south arc that passes through the nadir and zenith.

If you take out your pocket compass and use it to find due north and now turn to face the north, you are facing 0 degrees azimuth. Your right hand is facing east, at an azimuthal reading of 90 degrees. South, behind you, is at 180 degrees azimuth, and your left hand coincides with an azimuth of 270 degrees.

COORDINATE SYSTEM ACTIVITY

Creating an Alt–Az Star Chart

The fledgling urban astronomer can gain some experience with astronomical coordinate systems by using a compass and the star maps and planet chart in Appendices 1 and 6. You could go outside on a clear evening with a watch, compass, and appropriate finding chart. After locating one or two of the brighter sky objects, you might wish to keep track of their variation in azimuth and altitude as the evening progresses. The azimuth of a sky object, once again, is found by using the compass. You can estimate the altitude of the sky object by remembering that the overhead point (or zenith) is at 90 degrees and the horizon is at an altitude of 0 degrees. ■

Although the alt–az system can be used to locate celestial objects at the time of sighting, it is really a terrestrially based system. For use with sky objects, astronomers generally use a number of celestial coordinate systems. These depend upon the celestial north and south poles, which are projections of Earth's poles up (or down) to the mythical celestial sphere. The projection of Earth's equator on this sphere is the Celestial Equator. Another curve of importance is the ecliptic, the path of the Sun and planets across the sky.

Celestial coordinates use analogies of terrestrial latitude and longitude. A star along the Celestial Equator has a celestial latitude, or declination, of 0 degrees. The north pole star, Polaris, has a declination very close to 90 degrees. If there were a south pole star, its declination would be −90 degrees.

By convention, 0 degrees longitude on Earth is the longitude (or north–south arc) passing through Greenwich, England. The zero point of the celestial longitude system (right ascension) is the springtime intersection of the ecliptic and the Celestial Equator (which is in the constellation Pisces). The right ascension of a sky object increases in the eastward direction, as measured from the appropriate point in the constellation Pisces.

As mentioned earlier, some telescopes are equipped with an electrical clock drive that follows the apparent motion of the heavens. To find faint objects with such an instrument, setting circles are often attached to the telescope. The observer can use these circles to zero in upon the coordinates of the celestial object that is being sought.

During most urban observing sessions, only relatively bright celestial objects are visible. Clock drives are not essential and setting circles are overkill. Instead, the urban astronomer first uses a compass to find true north and then uses a star chart to locate some of the brighter constellations and visible planets. Only after locating some celestial landmarks with the naked eye will the experienced urban astronomer begin the telescopic portion of a sky viewing session.

Some basic, seasonal star charts are presented in Appendix 6. These may be enough to get you started. Another form of star chart, marketed by The Astronomical Society of the Pacific, shows relative star and planet positions for a particular month and time of night. If you hold the chart over your head and face north, you should, after a little practice, be able to identify the planets and many of the constellations. Most planetariums market star wheels, which allow you to vary the time of year and night on the star chart as long as your latitude (on Earth) remains constant.

Most star charts and star wheels show objects as dim as visual apparent magnitude 3 and are quite adequate for most urban settings. For dimmer objects, you may wish to consult a star atlas. Excellent star atlases are advertised in the pages of *Astronomy* and *Sky & Telescope* magazines.

Many star atlas publishers update their product periodically to correct for precession, a very long-period Earth motion. For most purposes, however, a good star atlas will provide a lifetime of service.

The planetarium is an excellent tool for practicing recognition of constellation patterns. Most cities have one or more large planetariums that offer regularly scheduled shows for the general public. In addition, many schools and universities are equipped with smaller planetariums.

If you consult the pages of *Astronomy* and *Sky & Telescope* magazines, you will see that a number of manufacturers advertise fully equipped portable planetariums for under $10,000. Outfitted with inflatable domes large enough to accommodate 30 people and projectors displaying hundreds of northern stars, these units are testimonies to modern technological ingenuity.

Most urban stargazers, alas, will not have enough spare cash to invest in one of these sophisticated devices. Never fear! Very inexpensive devices allowing the user to project constellation patterns on a ceiling at home are also available and are advertised in *Astronomy* and *Sky & Telescope.*

TELESCOPE ACTIVITY
Making Friends with Your Scope

Many novice astronomers are so enthusiastic about their new telescope that they take it out at night before they become acquainted with it during the day. This haste can really dampen their initial zeal.

To prevent such an unhappy evening, you should first spend a few hours during the day practicing on observing distant terrestrial objects. If your telescope is equipped with a spotting scope, you might first wish to bore-sight this with your lowest-power eyepiece on a very distant television antenna or building spire.

Follow the manufacturer's directions and then focus the spotting scope on the target. Move the telescope until the object is centered in the spotting scope. Then view the object through the low-power eyepiece. If the object is not centered in the telescope eyepiece, you should follow the manufacturer's instructions to realign the spotting scope. When you finally get it right, you should progress to higher-power eyepieces.

As well as helping with instrument alignment, this exercise will give you experience in changing eyepieces. When you are observing a sky object, you will generally want to start with a low-magnification, high-F.O.V. eyepiece. After you have located and centered the object in the eyepiece, you can change to the next-highest magnification. With practice, you will be able to do this without jarring the telescope tube excessively and losing the celestial object.

Many reflecting telescopes are equipped with aligning screws that allow you to shift the position of the primary mirror. If alignment is perfect, the focus image of a star will resemble a brilliant point of light. An asymmetrical stellar image resembling a comma indicates that mirror alignment may be necessary. Again, read the manufacturer's manual carefully. With practice, you may be able to realign the primary mirror by touch without interrupting your observing session.

When you are observing, it is always a good idea to let the telescope adjust to the environmental (or ambient) temperature. On particularly warm or cool nights, this adjustment time is from 30 to 40 minutes. See how the image quality improves as your telescope adjusts!

CHAPTER 4

Goddess of the Night

Slowly, silently now the moon
Walks the night in her silver shoon;
This way, and that, she peers and sees
Silver fruit upon silver trees.
—Walter de la Mare, *Silver* (1920)

The Moon, Earth's single natural satellite, has a strong hold on our psyches and imaginations. It is the favored target of most amateur astronomers—novices and seasoned veterans alike. More than a few professional astronomers, as well, point their larger instruments in its direction during their off-duty moments (although they may rarely confess this to their more jaded colleagues).

You may plan your evening sky viewing sessions around the visible planets, constellations, double or variable stars, or deep-sky objects. But inevitably, as you move your binoculars or telescope from one celestial target to another, your attention will drift back to the Moon. Invariably, when the Moon is above the horizon, it will be the "star" of any sky observation session.

Bright and prominent, the Moon is an especially good target for urban astronomers. The monthly variations, or phases, of our planet's one natural satellite are easy to observe with binoculars or telescope.

MOONWATCH ACTIVITY 1

Phases of the Moon Considered

To understand the phases of our Moon, draw a picture (like Figure 4-1) of the Earth–Moon system viewed from above (or below). Because the Sun is quite far away (about 93 million miles), rays of sunlight can be represented as a series of parallel lines. Draw several positions of the Moon along the circle representing its path around Earth. If you shade the Moon to represent bright and dark parts (the hemispheres exposed and not exposed to sunlight) and imagine viewing these from a location on Earth's surface, you will gain an immediate understanding of the lunar phases.

In performing this activity, be sure to shade that hemisphere of the Moon that is not exposed to sunlight. The *new moon* occurs when the Moon is between Earth and the Sun; the *full moon* occurs when Earth is between the Moon and the Sun. The lines between Earth and the *first* and *third quarter moons* make 90-degree angles with the line

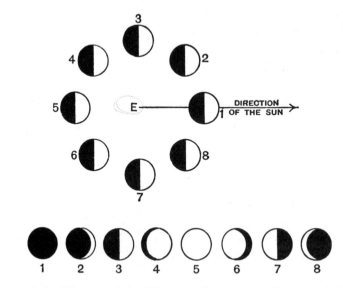

Figure 4-1 Phases of the Moon and corresponding Earth–Sun–Moon alignments (From A. Berry, *A Short History of Astronomy*. Courtesy Dover Publications, Inc.)

between Earth and the Sun. *Crescent moons* are intermediate between new and first/third quarter phases; *gibbous moons* are intermediate between full and first/third quarter phases.

When the unlit hemisphere of the Moon faces us, we experience a (1) new moon. As more and more of the illuminated portion of the Moon becomes visible, the phases evolve from (2) waxing crescent to (3) first quarter (when half of the Moon's sunlit side is visible). For another quarter cycle, the Moon continues to grow, or "wax." The "three-quarter" illuminated Moon is a (4) waxing gibbous, and this is followed by the (5) full moon. Then, for the next half of the lunar revolution, the Moon shrinks, or "wanes," through (6) waning gibbous, (7) third quarter, (8) waning crescent, and, once again, new moon.

As well as experimenting with lunar phases by using paper and pencil, you can gain an intuitive understanding of this phenomenon in a suitably darkened room by using a globe (or basketball) and a flashlight. In this activity, the flashlight represents the Sun; the spherical object stands in for the Moon; you, the observer, play the role of Earth. If you illuminate the "Moon" with "sunlight," you will notice that the Moon is fully illuminated when you are on the same side of the Moon as the Sun and is totally dark when you are exactly on the other side of it as the Sun. Try this activity to see what Sun–Moon–Earth alignments correspond with other lunar phases. ■

To theoretically explain the phases of the Moon, it is necessary to position the Sun a great distance from the Earth–Moon system, to assume that the Sun is larger than the Moon and that the Moon revolves around Earth. However, the monthly variations of the Moon should not be considered as proof of Earth's motion around the Sun. Actually, the now-discredited *geocentric cosmogony* (Earth-centered world view) of Aristotle and Ptolemy explains this phenomenon just as well as the correct *heliocentric cosmogony* (Sun-centered world view) developed by Copernicus and Kepler (which may have originated with the third-century B.C. Greek astronomer Aristarchus).

Because Earth moves around the Sun while the Moon is revolving around Earth, there are actually two lunar months! The *sidereal month* is the period of the Moon's revolution as measured against the distant stars. The *synodic month* is the Moon's cycle of phases, or its period with respect to the Sun. The sidereal period of the Moon's revolution is 27.3 days; the Moon's synodic period is 29.5 days. The lunar calendar month, or lunation, is identical to the synodic month.

It is easy to explore the lunar synodic and sidereal periods by using an astronomical computer program and a microcomputer. (Astronomical software for microcomputers is not expensive and is advertised in monthly astronomy magazines such as *Sky & Telescope* and *Astronomy*.) With such a software package, you can readily explore how long it takes the phases to repeat and how far the Moon shifts against the background of (apparently) fixed stars between each new or full moon. If you have access to a planetarium, you can also investigate these two lunar cycles without going outdoors.

MOONWATCH ACTIVITY 2

Phases of the Moon Observed

Investigation of the lunar cycles using direct observation is much more fun. To do this, go outside when the Moon is at the peak of the full phase. During the early evening, sketch the Moon and the stars nearest to it. Be sure to record the time. You should repeat the exercise for various other lunar phases during the monthly cycle, at least until the next full moon. The shift in lunar position relative to the much more distant stars should be evident after one or two phase cycles.

Almost any urban viewing site will offer you the opportunity of viewing the Moon at some phase of its monthly cycle. Sometimes, you will even be able to see it during the day.

The new moon rises at sunrise and sets at sunset. This phase is not observable.

In the waxing crescent phase, the Moon rises in the morning and sets in the evening. You will need good western exposure to observe the waxing crescent moon low in the sky at sunset.

First quarter moons rise at noon and set at midnight. In this phase, the Moon is highest in the sky at sunset and is therefore an easy target for the urban astronomer.

As the Moon matures toward the waxing gibbous phase, it rises in the afternoon and sets in the predawn sky. It will be highest in the sky during your early evening prime-observing time.

The full moon rises at sundown and sets at sunset. In the early evening, look for this phase in the eastern sky. This phase is highest in the sky at midnight.

Shrinking once again, the waning gibbous moon rises in the evening and sets in the morning. Look for it in the eastern sky around midnight.

The third quarter moon rises at midnight and sets at noon. Early-bird astronomers will see it low in the east in the predawn sky.

Finally, the waning crescent moon rises just before dawn and sets in the early afternoon. This phase is hard to observe from an urban site. ■

The modern month is, of course, not synchronized with lunar phases. A "blue moon" refers to a month with two full moons. In roughly one calendar year of every three, there will be a thirteenth full moon. In the year 1999, the months of January and March will each have two full moons.

Although ancient Greek astronomy was able to derive the correct explanation for lunar phases, it was not able to contend with the problem of tides. Even though ancient people correctly deduced a connection between Moon motions and oceanic tides, the correct explanation for this phenomenon awaited the physics of Sir Isaac Newton.

The Moon and the Tides

To gain an intuitive understanding of the Moon's effect on ocean and atmosphere tides, consider three points in Earth's ocean (as in Figure 4–2). One point is directly below the Moon (the sublunar point, with the Moon directly overhead at the zenith); the second

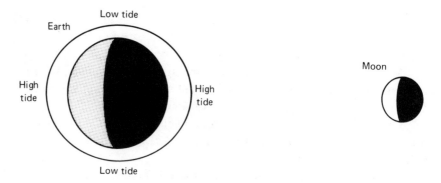

Figure 4-2 Tides in Earth's oceans produced by the Moon

point is exactly on the other side of Earth from the Moon (with the Moon directly under the observer's feet at the nadir); and the third point is at an intermediate location in the world ocean.

The gravitational pull of the Moon varies directly with the Moon's mass and decreases with the square of the Moon's distance. The sublunar water will therefore experience the greatest lunar attraction; the water on Earth's opposite side from the Moon will experience the least lunar attraction because it is the most distant from the Moon.

Thus, two water bulges or high tides will result. The water at the sublunar point will "lead the Earth," and the water on Earth's opposite side will bulge because it is "lagging the Earth."

Although universal gravitation is an inverse square phenomenon (meaning that the gravitational force decreases with the square of the distance to the center of the attracting body), any college physics student (and many high schoolers) can demonstrate that the tides decrease with the cube of the distance to the attracting object. The Moon is 2 to 3 times as significant in producing tides as is the Sun. The Sun's much greater mass is more than compensated for by the fact that our Moon is a much closer celestial neighbor.

The greatest variation in water level between low and high tides occurs when the Moon and Sun pull along the same line; tidal variation is minimized when they pull at right angles. Of course, other astronomical and geographical factors are also at play in determining local tides. These include local topography and variations in Moon–Earth and Sun–Earth distances.

MOONWATCH ACTIVITY 3

The Tides

A number of tide-related activities can be performed if you live near or visit a large body of water. By observing the position of the Moon in the sky, you can approximate when it is most nearly directly overhead or directly under your feet. These times should roughly correspond to the two daily high tides; the time exactly in between them is low tide. Try predicting in this fashion the times of high and low tide and compare your predictions to local tide tables published in the daily newspapers. If the predicted and tabulated times widely differ, you might wish to investigate the effects of local topography on tidal predictions. Also, you might wish to consider whether there is a lag time between predicted and actual high tides.

The most extreme tides should occur during full and new moons, when the Sun and Moon pull in the same direction. If you have access to a large body of water, you might wish to correlate the difference between high and low tides with lunar phase by directly measuring high- and low-water lines. Once again, by working at a number of waterfront sites, you can estimate the effects of local topography on the tidal range. ■

Details of the Earth–Moon System

For thousands of years, humans patiently observed lunar phases and motions with their naked eyes. Early telescopic astronomers confirmed what sharp-eyed pretelescopic people had long suspected: The Moon is tidally linked to Earth. Except for small variations, its period of rotation about its axis is identical to its period of revolution around Earth. Until the dawn of space travel allowed us to send spacecraft behind the Moon, we had direct knowledge of only one side of our natural satellite.

Galileo and his followers discovered craters and mountain ranges on the Moon's surface and large, comparatively flat and featureless regions that were dubbed *mare* (Latin for *sea*). We know today, of course, that the *maria* (plural for *seas*) are most likely the result of lava flows from very ancient geological processes (or selenological processes—from Selene, who was the ancient Greek moon goddess). Our Moon is too small to have long retained an atmosphere or ocean. Most or all of the craters were produced by impacts from comets and asteroids, probably billions of years in the past.

Approximately 25 percent of the Moon's surface is in the form of low-lying, relatively flat and dark maria. The brighter highlands constitute about 75 percent of our natural satellite's surface.

Because of the large size of our Moon relative to Earth (when compared with other satellites and their primaries in our Solar System), the Earth–Moon system is often considered to be a "double-planet" system. The Moon has about 1/82 the mass of Earth, and the Moon's radius of about 1,000 miles is roughly 1/4 Earth's radius. Most people are taught in school that the Moon circles Earth. In a strict sense, this is not quite correct. Actually, both objects circle a common center of mass located about 1,000 miles below Earth's surface.

Like most Solar System objects, the Moon's orbit is slightly elliptical. At its closest approach to Earth, or perigee, the Moon is roughly 222,000 miles from Earth's center. At its greatest distance from Earth, or apogee, the Moon is about 253,000 miles from Earth's center. The average distance of the Moon from Earth's surface is roughly 232,000 miles.

MOONWATCH ACTIVITY 4

The Angular Size of the Moon

If your telescope is equipped with a reticle eyepiece (an eyepiece containing concentric rings that allow you to measure the angular extent of a celestial object), you can readily approximate the angle subtended by (or covered by) the full moon. Using elementary trigonometry, you can use this information to estimate the distance to our natural satellite. The equation utilized in such an exercise is:

$$\text{Distance (miles)} = \frac{\text{Lunar diameter (miles)}}{\text{Sin (angle subtended by Moon)}}$$

For greatest accuracy, use the "exact" lunar diameter of 2,100 miles. To compare your results with the published lunar distances in *Sky & Telescope,* which are in kilometers, multiply your estimate (in miles) by 0.62. ∎

The brightest visual apparent magnitude of the Moon, when the Moon is full and at perigee, is −12.7. Although the amount of illumination reaching us from the full moon is only 1/500,000 the amount reaching us from the Sun, moonlight is still strong enough to cast shadows. If the Moon were a more reflective object (it only reflects 7 percent of the incident sunlight back into space), the Moon would be considerably brighter than it is.

Just as the Moon produces tides on Earth, the larger body affects the orbit of the satellite. Because of this interplay, the average orbital separation of the two worlds is not constant over very long periods of geologic time. When the Sun has evolved to the red giant phase (about 5,000 million years in the future), the Moon will have receded from Earth to the point that the lunar month will be about twice as long as it is today.

Intensive investigation of lunar samples returned by Apollo astronauts and Soviet robots have cleared up some of the mystery regarding the Moon's origin. Before the advent of space travel, it was unclear whether the Moon had formed independently of Earth and been captured by the gravitational pull of the larger object, coalesced in current state as a satellite of Earth, or fissioned from the larger object. The Moon solidified 4.6 to 4.7 billion years ago, and an early Earth–Moon association is favored by many researchers. Evidence for an Earth–Moon association that began early in the history of the Solar System has been found in studies of the distribution of chemical elements in the Moon's crust. Apparently, a melting and chemical separation in the lunar crust occurred about

4.4 billion years ago, only 200 million years or so after the origin of the Solar System. This event might be due to the capture of the Moon by our planet.

Another famous controversy of the 1950s and 1960s is whether the craters and maria of the Moon are predominantly due to impacts or volcanism. A compromise between these two extreme viewpoints seems to have been arrived at. Most of the craters (which vary in size from a few inches to more than 100 miles across) were formed by impacts. Analysis of space and Earth-based observations has not turned up clear evidence of volcanic craters on the Moon. At least some of the maria, however, seem to be remnants of basins that were filled with lava early in the Moon's history. The outgassed lava may have been heated by the decay of radioactive materials within the early Moon's crust.

Most of these volatile outgassed materials have long since evaporated from the lunar soil. However, there is some possibility that deposits of frozen water still exist in the polar highlands of the Moon, in craters and crevasses not exposed to direct sunlight. Needless to say, knowing the location of such deposits would be a boon to future lunar colonists.

The Observable Moon

One beautiful sky phenomenon associated with the Moon (and also with the Sun) is the halo. A halo is a circular ring of 22- or 46-degree radius that is caused by scattering and refraction of moonlight by high-altitude ice crystals in terrestrial cirrus clouds. Under certain conditions, two halos are visible, both centered upon the Moon. The characteristics of the lunar halo are best explained by the theory of light scattering by high-altitude ice crystals in Earth's atmosphere.

Another striking naked-eye lunar phenomenon is earthshine. When the Moon is in or near its new phase, sunlight can be refracted through Earth's atmosphere, strike the Moon's dark surface, and be reflected back to Earth. Even the tiny percentage of the refracted/reflected sunlight that reaches the observer's eyes is sometimes sufficient to render the outline of the new moon dimly visible. A very young crescent moon superimposed upon a barely visible lunar sphere illuminated by earthshine is called by some "the New Moon in the Arms of the Old."

MOONWATCH ACTIVITY 5

The Moon through Binoculars

With binoculars having a 5X–10X power magnification, a range of lunar phenomena become observable. The dividing line between the bright and dark regions of the Moon (the terminator) stands out in stark relief. The larger of the dark maria can be easily distinguished from the brighter highlands. The best time to view the Moon is not during the full phase, when the intense glare makes discernment of detail difficult and no shadows are cast by lunar features, but shortly after the first quarter phase. The shadows of some of the larger walled craters and mountain ranges will then be clearly visible through binoculars. ∎

With even a small telescope, many additional features become visible (Figure 4–3). But remember, when compared with the binocular image, the telescope image will be upside down, or inverted.

If you use a 3- to 4-inch aperture telescope and a 30X–75X power magnification, many peaks, craters, and rills become observable as do all the maria. Under ideal viewing conditions, even a 10X–20X power magnification will reveal lunar features as small as 15 or 20 miles across.

MOONWATCH ACTIVITY 6

The Moon through a Telescope

A number of interesting telescope lunar activities are fun to perform by the novice (or more advanced) observer. You might wish to

Figure 4–3a West Hemisphere of the Moon as viewed through a small telescope

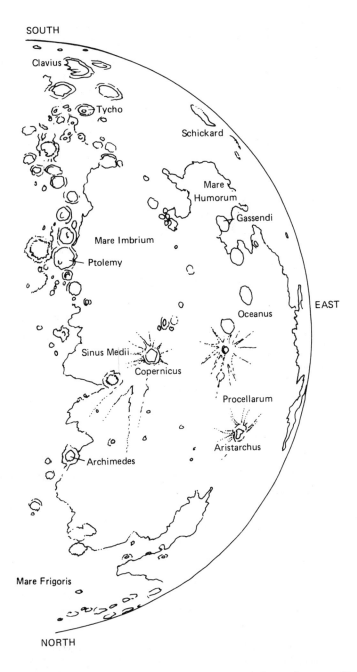

Figure 4-3b East Hemisphere of the Moon as viewed through a small tele-scope

69

concentrate upon the shadow cast across the lunar surface by one prominent elevated feature such as a mountain or crater wall. By sketching the shadow on the surrounding terrain over a period of one synodic period, you will gain an appreciation of the effects of phases upon apparent lunar relief. Once again, a reticle eyepiece will allow you to obtain a quantitative measure of lunar-feature shadow length.

For best results, choose a feature that is visible during crescent, half, and full phases. The walls of one of the easily found craters such as Tycho or Copernicus might be good targets for this activity. With the aid of the reticle eyepiece, you can track the variation in crater-wall shadow length as the Moon ages.

Careful lunar cartography both from space and Earth yielded accurate heights for the lunar mountain ranges before the first Apollo craft touched down in Mare Tranquillitatis in 1969. Before this effort, it was suspected that some mountains on the Moon's near side might rival Mount Everest. It is now known that quite a few lunar mountains are 20,000 feet or more above the surrounding plains. One peak in the Leibnitz Mountains, located on the south limb of the Moon, towers 30,000 feet above the surrounding terrain.

Some of the great walled craters also rise to dizzying heights above the lunar plains. Clavius, which is 145 miles in diameter, has 12,000-foot-high walls and contains 17,000-foot-high mountains. Copernicus, which is 56 miles in diameter, is also ringed by 12,000-foot-high walls.

The crater Tycho, also equipped with 12,000-foot-high walls, is 50 miles in diameter and is the finest example of a "rayed" crater on the Moon. At full moon, Tycho is the most prominent lunar crater. Rays are thought to be secondary impact features formed when a high-speed object slammed into the Moon in the very distant past and molten lunar material was ejected outward. Some of the material ejected in such impacts may have escaped the Moon and actually reached Earth. This is a favored origin for a class of meteoritic objects called *tektites*.

Using Figure 4–3 as a guide, you can point your telescope or binoculars at the Moon and soon become familiar with a number of lunar features. Different features are apparent at various lunar phases. One key in identifying a feature is the location of the terminator, the boundary between light and dark portions of the lunar disk.

In the young waxing crescent moon, only the western edge of our satellite is illuminated. Moving from north to south along the terminator, you will easily locate Mare Crisium and Mare Fecunditatis. Shadows point toward the east. Because of the length of the shadows, features stand out in good relief.

As the Moon ages toward the first quarter phase, the terminator crosses (moving north to south once again) Mare Nectaris and Mare Tranquillitatis. The astronauts of Apollo 11 landed in Mare Tranquillitatis in 1969; those of Apollo 16 later touched down near Mare Nectaris. Then, a bit south of the equator and east of Mare Nectaris, you will notice the terminator on the 65-mile-wide crater Theophilus. This crater has 18,000-foot walls and a central mountain. A bit southeast of Theophilus are two other large craters, Cyrillus and Catharina.

Just before the first quarter phase, the terminator crosses the great walled plain Hipparchus. This striking object is 100 miles across. Those walls still standing are about 4,000 feet high. Farther north, the terminator lies on the eastern fringe of Mare Serenitatis, the great walled plains Eudoxus and Aristoteles, and Mare Frigoris. The astronauts of the final Apollo mission, Apollo 17, landed in the Fra Mauro Highlands between Mare Serenitatis and Mare Tranquillitatis.

At the first quarter phase, the terminator crosses Sinus Medii, a small dark plain at the center of the lunar disk. Contrast will begin decreasing as the Moon ages toward the full phase. Shadows of surface features shorten and relief becomes less apparent.

Shortly after the first quarter phase, the terminator crosses Archimedes, a 50-mile diameter walled plain in Mare Imbrium. In the waxing gibbous phase, the terminator crosses the great walled crater Copernicus, just north of the Moon's equator.

As the Moon approaches the full phase, the terminator crosses Mare Humorum. At the full moon, this "sea" seems to be sprinkled with white spots. These might be due to sunlight bouncing off the remains of very ancient lava flows.

Just before the full moon, the terminator crosses Oceanus Procellarum, a great dark plain, and the crater Aristarchus. As discussed later, this crater is a subject of active research.

During the full phase, surface contrast is at a minimum because of the absence of shadows. After the full moon, the terminator line lies on the west of the disk. Now pointed west, the shadows lengthen and contrast improves. The first objects to disappear on the face of the aging Moon are the first that appeared on the young Moon—the western "seas," Mare Crisium and Mare Fecunditatis. ■

If you get bored simply looking at the Moon, you can always join the search for *transient lunar phenomena* (abbreviated TLP). These events are characterized by temporary and localized brightenings of portions of the lunar surface. A TLP event might last for a few minutes or a few hours. Observers have reported these sporadic episodes, which sometimes include color variations, since the late eighteenth century.

One of the prime centers of TLP is the ringed crater Aristarchus, which is 28 miles in diameter and has 9,000-foot-high rim walls. Located near the Moon's northeast limb, this feature seems to glow brightly when the Moon is in the waxing crescent phase. Although some of the glow might be due to earthlight striking an intrinsically bright feature, orbiting Apollo command modules detected more radon gas associated with Aristarchus than with any other lunar feature. This radioactive gas might be emitted during a TLP event.

Transient lunar phenomena have been observed at locations other than Aristarchus and seem to be best viewed in the blue or violet range of the spectrum. Although the mechanisms for TLP are not completely understood, most astronomers acknowledge that they are not illusory. Probably, some lunar volatiles (such as radon gas) are produced in pockets of undecayed radioactive material. Future miners of the Moon should carefully remember the reported locations of TLP events!

MOONWATCH ACTIVITY 7

Hunting for TLP Events

If you have an urban viewing site that is reasonably dark and a small telescope, you can join the search for TLP events. Participation in this activity requires blue or violet filters for your telescope (to increase the contrast between the TLP emissions and the surrounding terrain), some familiarity with lunar features, and a great deal of patience!

You should approach your TLP hunt with the attitude of a very patient explorer. With a great deal of luck, you might observe a TLP event on your first night out. However, you could easily observe for a lifetime with no success. ■

Most celestial objects have a very small angular extent. The stars and even the naked-eye planets are essentially bright points in the sky. Because the Moon is an extended object (about 1/2 degree of arc), stars will often pass behind, or be occulted by, the Moon. A grazing occultation, in which a bright star is just occulted by mountains on the Moon's limb, can be used by teams of amateurs, equipped with good telescopes and timers, to estimate more accurately the heights of lunar mountains. Stars involved in grazing occultations and the best viewing locations in the United States are reported in a celestial calendar published annually in the monthly magazine *Sky & Telescope*.

MOONWATCH ACTIVITY 8

Participating in an Occultation Event

To participate in an occultation event, it is best to collaborate with astronomers in a number of locations, all of whom have synchronized their timepieces. You should record your exact location and, as accurately as possible, the times that the star disappears behind the Moon and reappears. If it puts in several reappearances during a grazing occultation, these times are even more valuable in determining lunar local topographic variations.

To understand the importance of observations of lunar grazing occultations, consider the following illustration. If a star that you are viewing disappears behind a feature on the lunar limb and reappears 1.5 seconds later, you can determine the size of the lunar feature from the lunar orbital speed around Earth. Since the Moon circles Earth at an average velocity of just over 1 kilometer (0.62 mile) per second, the lunar feature occulting the star has a width of about 1.5 kilometers (0.93 mile). ■

73

Photo Gallery

The pictures in this photo gallery were taken by John Pazmino of the Amateur Astronomers Association of New York between 1972 and 1982. These images, from urban sites within the boroughs of Brooklyn and Manhattan in New York City, are representative of the astronomical photography you can accomplish, using modest equipment, from an urban location. If you wish to learn more about astronomical photography, you might start by consulting Appendix 12.

The cameras used by Mr. Pazmino were 35-mm models equipped with a variety of lenses. These cameras were not mounted on telescopes.

The images presented here were converted to black and white from color slides. Standard daylight slide film and processing techniques were used. During each exposure, which had a duration of a few seconds to a minute, the camera was mounted on a tripod. This accomplished the objective of steady camera aim during the exposure. An inexpensive cable release was applied to trip the shutter.

Exposure times much longer than a minute should not be attempted unless the camera is mounted on a clock drive, as described in Appendix 12. If you were to attempt long exposure times without the use of a clock drive, star images would be replaced by linear trails.

If you decide to try your hand at urban astronomical photography, be prepared to waste the first dozen or so exposures. Keep a good log of the exposure times, films, and lenses used to photograph each celestial object. You will soon know what works and what does not and will become adept at obtaining good photos of the Moon, naked-eye planets, and brighter stars.

Lunar Eclipse over Queens, photographed from the Empire State
Building, Manhattan; November 18, 1975.

Procyon, Moon, Saturn, Mars, Castor, and Pollux (left to right) over Brooklyn houses; May 5, 1976.

Venus over the World Trade Center and Woolworth Tower, Manhattan; January 18, 1972.

Jupiter, Spica, Saturn, and Mars (left to right) over Manhattan skyline; March 20, 1982.

CHAPTER 5

Wandering Stars:
The Planets of
Our Solar System

After an interval, reading here in the midnight,
With the great stars looking on—all the stars of
   Orion looking,
And the Pleiades—and the duo looking of Saturn
   and ruddy Mars;
Pondering, reading my own songs, after a long
   interval, (sorrow and death familiar now,)
Ere closing the book, what pride! what joy! to find
   them,
Standing so well the test of death and night!
And the duo of Saturn and Mars!
   —Walt Whitman, *After an Interval* (November 22,
      1825): *Midnight—Saturn & Mars in Conjunction*

The earliest astronomers concentrated upon the apparent motions of the Sun and Moon. Good reasons exist for the almost exclusive early interest in these celestial bodies. When it comes to keeping track of seasonal variations and developing a calendar that is reasonably constant, diurnal (daily) and annual motions of the Sun and the monthly variations of lunar phases are most significant. The rest of the celestial pantheon can be viewed as a mere tableau upon which the humanly important drama of the Sun and Moon takes place.

Later in the history of astronomy, around 3,000 years ago, observers began to concentrate upon the motions of the "wandering stars," or planets. To initial naked-eye observers, these were divine objects circling a stationary Earth. Only a few centuries ago did the telescope confirm that these wanderers are actually worlds in their own right and that, like the Earth, they circle the Sun.

Planetary Motions

All of the naked-eye planets and the more recently discovered outer worlds Uranus and Neptune follow the ecliptic, or path of the

Sun around the sky. This occurs because these objects circle the Sun within 7 degrees of the same plane. Only distant Pluto, probably the smallest world in the Solar System as well as the coldest, has a sizable inclination (17 degrees) from the plane of the ecliptic. Pluto also has the most elliptical orbit in the Solar System. Because its perihelion, or closest point to the Sun, is within the orbit of Neptune (normally the eighth planet) and Pluto is now near perihelion, it is currently the eighth planet from the Sun, not the ninth.

In the modern model of the Solar System (which can be regarded as proven after three decades of successful interplanetary probes), the planets revolve around the Sun in nearly circular elliptical orbits. Viewed from the side, the Solar System is an essentially disk-shaped object centered upon the Sun.

Although Copernicus had replaced the much earlier view held by the ancient Greek astronomer Ptolemy (in which the planets and Sun circled Earth) with a sun-centered, or heliocentric, world view, he still maintained that planetary orbits around the Sun were perfectly circular. Kepler, using naked-eye observations of Tycho Brahe, finally demonstrated in the early seventeenth century that planetary orbits are actually elliptical.

All of the planets move in more or less elliptical orbits around the Sun. Kepler's laws of elliptical motion also state correctly that a planet speeds up when it is closest to the Sun and that the square of the period of revolution (or year) of a planet increases with the cube of its average distance from the Sun. Kepler's laws and Galileo's telescopic observations are the solid bedrocks upon which Isaac Newton founded the discipline of classical physics.

Planet Types

There are two basic planet types in the Solar System. Worlds close to the Sun, which include Mercury, Venus, Earth, and Mars, tend to be small, dense, and rocky. The atmospheres of these *terrestrial* worlds are relatively thin, and they possess few or no satellites. Farther out from the solar furnace are the *gas giant* worlds, also called the *Jovians*. These planets, which include Jupiter, Saturn, Uranus, and Neptune, tend to be less dense and larger than the terrestrial worlds. They possess thick atmospheres of hydrogen, helium, methane, and ammonia, and they have many satellites. Although only the rings of Saturn are visible through small earth-bound telescopes, the *Voyager* robot space probes have found less visible rings encircling all of the gas giant worlds.

Pluto swings around the Sun in a highly elliptical orbit and is usually (although not for the next few years) the outermost planet. Although it is small and difficult to observe and is the only major body in the Solar System not yet visited by a robotic emissary from Earth, many scientists believe that Pluto may be an escaped satellite of Neptune, which is at present the outermost planet from the Sun. If an early interstellar probe makes a side trip past Pluto in the first quarter of the twenty-first century, we will know a great deal more about this strange and frigid world.

Although observational data is far from conclusive at the present time, some astronomers believe that a third planet type will be found circling some stars in the Sun's interstellar neighborhood. These *brown dwarfs* would be more massive than the gas giants but less massive than stars. It is possible that a brown dwarf's surface, heated by the slow gravitational contraction of the planetary material, could be considerably higher than that of planets closer to the primary star.

We can gain some understanding of the distribution of planets in the Solar System by considering the origin of the Sun, Earth, and planets. According to current theories, our Solar System began to condense from an interstellar cloud of dust and gas called a *nebula* around five billion years ago. Consisting of mostly hydrogen and helium, the nebular material had been "doped" with impurities of heavier elements by outgassing from a nearby exploding supernova star. As supernova material interacted with the nebula that eventually became the Solar System, the ensuing turbulence may have triggered contraction of the cloud.

As this primeval nebula contracted, some of the gaseous material began to contract into the protoplanets and protosun. Those celestial icebergs we call *comets* condensed more than a trillion miles from the protosun.

Initially, all of the planets must have been Jovians. The hydrogen/helium constitution of these newborn worlds would have mirrored the infant Sun.

As more and more material gathered in the center of the nebula, temperatures and pressures near the core of the infant Sun began to rise. A milestone was reached when the ignition conditions for thermonuclear fusion (the conversion of hydrogen to helium and energy) were achieved within the solar interior.

Very quickly (from the cosmic point of view), the Sun turned on. As electromagnetic radiation streamed from our infant primary star, the inner portions of the solar nebula heated up. Simultaneously, radiation pressure from the sunlight pushed the gas and dust of the solar nebula out of the inner Solar System.

The hydrogen/helium atmospheres of the inner planets would have been evaporated within thousands of years or less. The primeval atmospheres of the gas giants were preserved only because of the greater distances of these planets from the Sun.

But there were still plenty of comets floating around in the inner Solar System. Some of these impacted the inner planets, producing atmospheres of carbon dioxide, nitrogen, and water vapor. These cometary atmospheres were supplemented by volcanoes that erupted as the inner planets cooled.

Because Mercury was the closest planet to the Sun and was rather small, it was unable to hold its cometary or outgassed atmosphere. Any thin atmosphere that is maintained today by this hot, small world is principally due to the stream of ionized matter always flowing out from the Sun—the solar wind.

Venus, a near twin of Earth in terms of mass, is about 30 percent closer to the Sun. Its volcanic outgassing may have been temperature driven and therefore proceeded faster than that of Earth. The rapid buildup of carbon dioxide in this planet's atmosphere resulted in a dense, "greenhouse" atmosphere that greatly increased the surface temperature of Venus. Temperatures are far above the boiling point of water on Venus. Thus, life could never get a toehold there and water remains in the atmosphere as water vapor rather than forming liquid oceans.

About 50 percent farther from the Sun than Earth and somewhat smaller is "the Red Planet," Mars. The atmosphere of Mars is still evolving. Giant volcanoes such as Nix Olympica may erupt at million-year intervals, and much of the planet's water may be locked in the frozen soil as permafrost. Mars has a thin atmosphere that is composed mostly of carbon dioxide, although some water and oxygen are present on this planet. The consensus among astronomers is that there are no indigenous Martians. We may, however, begin to transfer some representatives of the terrestrial ecology to Mars in the next century.

Observable Planets

With a good pair of binoculars or a small telescope, observations of Venus, Mars, Jupiter, and Saturn can be most rewarding (Figure 5–1). You may not have much luck in seeing Mercury because of its proximity to the Sun. Only in the crisp autumn skies of regions such as rural New England will you be most likely to catch a glimpse of this fleet "Messenger of the Gods."

Because the naked-eye planets are all confined to the plane of the ecliptic, they will seem to ride a track through the same band of constellations—the zodiac. To find the zodiacal position of Venus, Mars, Jupiter, and Saturn between the years 1991 and 2000, consult the planetary ephemeris in Appendix 1. This information should be used in conjunction with the seasonal star charts in Appendix 6.

In the urban evening sky, you can often observe one or more of these worlds shortly after sunset if your view is not blocked by a tall building. Through binoculars, the disks of the naked-eye planets can usually be resolved, as can the rings of Saturn. A 3- to 4-inch aperture (primary lens or mirror diameter) telescope is usually necessary to resolve planetary features. A maximum magnification of 100X (100 times) is adequate for many urban-viewing planetary purposes, although higher magnification is better for monitoring surface and atmospheric conditions on Mars.

Venus

At its brightest, Venus has a visual magnitude of about −4. It is then more than 6 times brighter than the brightest star, Sirius, which has a visual magnitude of −1.46.

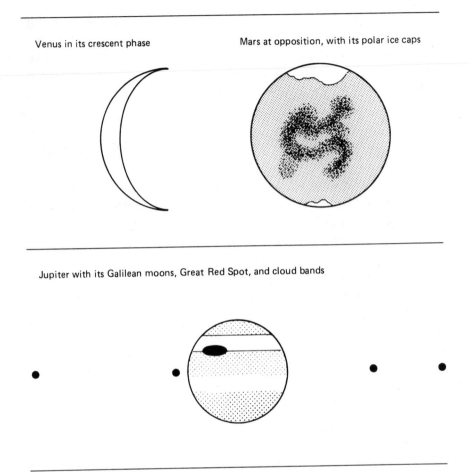

Venus in its crescent phase

Mars at opposition, with its polar ice caps

Jupiter with its Galilean moons, Great Red Spot, and cloud bands

Saturn and its rings

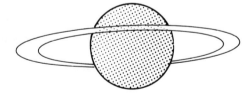

Figure 5–1 Drawings of the four easily observable naked-eye planets as they appear through a small telescope during fair-to-good seeing conditions.

Venus, like Mercury, is an "inferior planet," one that is closer to the Sun than is Earth. Unlike the "superior planets," those worlds that are farther from the Sun than is Earth, inferior planets show phases.

VENUS ACTIVITY

Charting the Phases and Angular Size

The phases of Venus are easily observable through urban skies. An interesting activity for the amateur urban astronomer is to observe the phases of Venus and chart them as the planet moves around the Sun. A good time for this activity is shortly after sunset when Venus is an "evening star" in the western sky or shortly before dawn when Venus is a "morning star" in the east.

If your telescope is equipped with a reticle eyepiece, you can monitor variations in the planet's angular extent as its phases change. Venus will appear largest when it is between Earth and the Sun and is, consequently, very difficult to observe. ∎

Venus has no known natural satellites, although some robots from Earth have taken up residence above the cloud banks. The period of rotation, or day, of this planet is 243 earth-days. The period of revolution around the Sun, or year, for Venus is 224 earth-days. Unlike Earth, the rotation and revolution directions of Venus are opposite from each other.

From the point of view of the earthbound amateur observer, it seems to make little difference whether Venus is observed through a good pair of binoculars or a small telescope. Even through the 20-inch aperture refractor at the Van Vleck Observatory, Wesleyan University, Middletown, Connecticut, the aspect presented by this planet is featureless clouds.

Just after inferior conjunction, when the planet is nearly in line with Earth and the Sun, some amateur astronomers have observed a Venusian atmospheric phenomenon called the *ashen light.* Through a telescope with an aperture between 2 and 5 inches, some observers have reported this peculiar brownish red hue to the unilluminated portion of the planet's disk. Very difficult to observe in the problematic urban skies, this may be related to some auroral or lightning effect in the Venusian atmosphere.

At some point in the very distant future, we may attempt to modify or "terraform" this planet's atmosphere by using some variety of genetically engineered terrestrial microorganism. Until and unless this is done, about all we can hope for is to continue to enjoy the beautiful spectacle of the changing phases of this morning or evening star through our binoculars or telescopes.

The best times to observe Venus are generally within a few hours after sunset and a few hours before dawn. Because Venus will usually be seen low in the western dusk sky or eastern predawn sky, local light pollution will probably render observation of the ashen light impossible. However, because this planet is the brightest object in the sky after the Sun and Moon, the phases of Venus can be observed on any clear night when the planet is visible.

Mars

While Venus is relatively boring for the amateur observer, the same is certainly not true of Mars. At its closest approach (opposition) to Earth, this reddish planet is a "mere" 35 million miles away. Almost from the dawn of telescopic astronomy, observers have been able to view seasonal changes on the Martian surface and the waxing or waning of the planet's polar caps.

Because of its greater distance from the Sun, Mars is colder than Earth and its year is longer. In fact, although the day of this planet is almost identical in length to that of Earth, it takes 687 days for Mars to revolve once around the Sun. Martian seasons, therefore, are about twice as long as their terrestrial counterparts.

Even today, after numerous robot expeditions have failed to find traces of Martian life, no planet is more connected in the public imagination with the idea of extraterrestrial life. Much of this interest can be traced to 1877, when the Italian astronomer Schiaparelli commented that he saw straight lines or channels on the surface of Mars through his telescope. American newspapers translated the Italian word for channels, *canali,* as *canals.* While astronomers such as the American Percival Lowell were mapping the apparent straight lines on Mars, science fiction writers such as H. G. Wells and Edgar Rice Burroughs were writing science fiction stories about the fading but still great Martian civilization.

In many of these tales, the canals were a planet-wide irrigation system designed to bring water from the polar caps to the great cities near the warmer equator of the planet. Martians viewed the young, vibrant Earth across the sea of space and plotted the invasion of our world. In 1938, when radio commentator Orson Welles presented a Halloween dramatization of the H. G. Wells's classic story of a Martian invasion, *War of the Worlds,* a great many people panicked.

Unfortunately, the canals are an optical illusion. Mars possesses enormous volcanoes, craters, mountains, and a rift valley that dwarfs the Grand Canyon, but no evidence has been found for even microscopic Martians. Within the next few decades, of course, there may well be Martians, but they will be transplanted humans from "the Third Planet."

Even before humans travel to Mars, there is a great deal for the amateur observer to see on this small planet. Mists and clouds of several types can be observed since the thin atmosphere of Mars does have a meteorology. During the mission of *Mariner IX* in 1971, earthbound observers did yeoman service in monitoring the progress of a planet-wide dust storm.

The Martian planet-wide dust storms form when the northern region of Mars is pointed toward the Sun (northern-hemisphere summer) and when the planet is closest to the Sun, near perihelion. Regional yellow clouds form quite rapidly under these circumstances and then diffuse to cover the entire planet. Martian surface features can then be obscured for weeks or months. Because intense winds are the agent for development of these dust storms, amateur astronomers can gain information regarding Martian atmospheric circulation by monitoring the yellow clouds in the planet's atmosphere.

MARS ACTIVITY 1

Observing the Red Planet's Meteorology

A 4.5- to 6-inch aperture telescope is sufficient to observe yellow clouds in the planet's atmosphere, with the aid of a red filter in front of the aperture. Blue clouds (probably mists or fogs near the surface) can be photographed with ultraviolet-sensitive film. Although exceptional urban-viewing conditions would be required to monitor the meteorology of this planetary neighbor, you could check up on the progress of large dust storms by observing night-to-night variations in the visibility of Martian surface features.

To check up on the development of a Martian dust storm, it is probably wise to consult *Astronomy* or *Sky & Telescope* magazines to obtain predictions of a forthcoming storm. Then, you could plan a regular observing program in which you might sketch the appearance of the planet's surface and any clouds that you might observe. As the storm progresses, more and more surface detail on Mars will disappear. ∎

Under a magnification of about 75X, the face of Mars looks about the same size as the Moon to the naked eye when Mars is closest to Earth. At its brightest, Mars has a visual apparent magnitude of –2.8; at its dimmest, its magnitude is about 3.

MARS ACTIVITY 2

Estimating Brightness and Size

An amateur urban astronomer could estimate the visual apparent magnitude of Mars on a particular date by comparing it with stars of known (and constant) magnitude. If your telescope is equipped with a reticle eyepiece, you can monitor changes in this planet's angular size as its position relative to Earth changes.

To estimate the visual apparent magnitude of Mars at any particular time, you will need an atlas or star map that presents visual apparent magnitudes of stars in the zodiacal constellations. If Mars seems a bit dimmer than magnitude 1 stars near it in the sky and a bit brighter than magnitude 2 stars, you can safely say that its visual apparent magnitude is between 1 and 2.

The reticle eyepieces available as accessories to many commercially available telescopes contain internal angular calibrations. By observing Mars for a series of nights and comparing it to the reticle eyepiece calibration, the urban astronomer can readily monitor the changes in the angular size of the planet's disk. ■

New York amateur astronomer Ralph Kantrowitz has communicated some hints for observing, from an urban location, detail on the Martian surface when this planet is closest to Earth. During the heating season, when warm thermals may cause air turbulence, try to observe at a site far from building chimneys and windows. In all seasons, allow roughly half an hour for your telescope to reach the outdoor temperature.

A good rule of thumb for maximum magnification for observing Mars from the city is 40X (40 times) per inch of telescope aperture. Yellow filters will provide the best overall view and provide the best contrast for observing dust storms. Orange filters are good for dark features on the planet's disk, while green or blue filters are recommended for observation of polar caps and clouds. Make sure that the filters you select have transmissions higher than 40 percent so as not to excessively diminish the light intensity from the planet. (A filter transmission of 40 percent means that 60 percent of the light reaching the filter is not transmitted to the observer's eye.)

The two small moons of Mars, Deimos and Phobos, are much too small to be visible in any amateur's telescope. But these airless bodies, which are most likely captured asteroids or comet nuclei, are ideally suited to serve as orbital base camps for the first human interplanetary expeditions.

With a good pair of binoculars, you can just resolve the planet's disk under good viewing conditions (although you will do better of course through a telescope). The prevailing red color, which is probably due to iron oxide in the planet's crust, is quite evident.

With a 6-inch aperture telescope, the polar caps can be observed under clear urban skies. Although some of the polar cap material is water, we now know that most of it is frozen carbon dioxide (or dry ice).

MARS ACTIVITY 3

Observing the Polar Caps

An urban astronomer can monitor Martian seasons by observing growth and shrinkage of the planet's polar caps. If your telescope is equipped with a reticle eyepiece, you can easily determine the angular extent of the polar caps relative to the angle subtended by the entire planet. Green or yellow filters are most useful in maximizing the contrast of the polar caps.

If your night-to-night observations reveal that the north polar cap of Mars is shrinking and the south polar cap is expanding, you know that the planet is experiencing northern summer and southern winter. Conversely, if the north polar cap seems to be expanding and the south polar cap is shrinking, the planet is in northern winter and southern summer. ∎

Although the Martian atmosphere is very thin and water is a precious commodity in this planetary desert, Mars has all the necessary ingredients for a self-sufficient human colony. Long before the year 2100, humans will probably be living there. Because of the comparatively small size of Mars, they will have to adjust to a surface gravity that is less than 40 percent that of Earth. Good training for a stint on this cold world might be a year or two in Antarctica.

Mars will be a sure-fire "star" of any observing session when this planet is in the sky. Because of its lower reflectivity and greater distance and the fact that it is a superior planet rather than an inferior planet, Mars is always dimmer than cloud-shrouded

Venus. For more information on the evening observability of Mars (and the other naked-eye planets), consult the planetary ephemeris in Appendix 1.

Jupiter

Jupiter is more than 5 times farther out from the Sun than is Earth. This enormous world thus requires about 12 years to revolve once around the Sun. With a cloudtop radius more than 10 times the radius of Earth and a mass 318 times greater than that of Earth, Jupiter is clearly "the King of the Planets."

At the present time, our space and ground observatories cannot detect the presence of earthlike planets circling nearby stars. The present-day threshold of detection is objects of Jovian mass since these will notably perturb the proper motions of nearly stars viewed across a field of much more distant stars.

For an object so large, Jupiter rotates surprisingly rapidly. Features in the equatorial cloudtops circle the planet in less than 10 hours. Because of Jupiter's gaseous nature, the rotation rate is a function of latitude.

At its brightest, the visual apparent magnitude of this giant world is −2.5. Although Jupiter has many satellites and a faint ring system, only its four largest satellites are visible in binoculars or a small telescope. Called the *Galilean moons* after their discoverer, these satellites are actually worlds in their own right.

JUPITER ACTIVITY 1

Observing the Galilean Moons

The brightest of the Galilean moons of Jupiter is Ganymede, at 5.1 magnitude. Io is slightly dimmer at 5.5 magnitude, and the apparent visual magnitude of Europa is 5.7 magnitude. Callisto, the dimmest of Jupiter's large satellites, has a visual apparent magnitude of 6.3. When all four of the Galilean moons are visible in your telescope's eyepiece, you could use their difference in magnitude to identify them. Under ideal (nonurban) conditions, a person with exceptionally fine vision may be able to pick out the three brightest Galilean moons with the naked eye. ∎

The satellites Ganymede and Callisto are considerably larger than our Moon. Ganymede, in fact, is slightly larger than the planet Mercury. *Voyager 1* and *Voyager 2* have returned a wealth of scientific data and photographs of these lovely worlds. Io's volcanoes, Europa's frozen seas, and surface markings on the other Galilean satellites are, unfortunately, not directly observable through an amateur's telescope.

JUPITER ACTIVITY 2

The Great Red Spot and Jovian Rotation

With a 4-inch aperture telescope, a number of features on Jupiter can be clearly resolved from an urban site. These include the latitudinal cloud bands and the mysterious Great Red Spot. Large enough to swallow several planets the size of Earth, this southern-hemisphere cloudtop feature has existed for at least three centuries. With a 6-inch telescope, the amateur can monitor conditions around the Great Red Spot.

One Jovian activity for an amateur urban astronomer equipped with a small telescope is the verification of Jupiter's 10-hour rotation period. You can do this by sketching the position of the Great Red Spot relative to the planet's disk during a several-hour observation session. ∎

JUPITER ACTIVITY 3
Satellite Occultations

Jovian events greatly favored by serious amateur astronomers are occultations of the Galilean moons. These occur when one of the satellites passes across, or transits, the visible face of the planet. The shadow of the moon can then be clearly observed as it crosses the face of the giant planet. During an occultation, a 5- or 6-inch telescope can resolve the disk of the Galilean moon.

Occultations of the Galilean moons are usually announced months in advance in *Sky & Telescope* and *Astronomy* magazines. Amateur observations of a satellite's disappearance and reappearance times and brightness variations as a moon is setting or rising are of use to professional astronomers studying planetary atmospheres. The monthly magazines just mentioned often contain information about coordination of occultation observations. ∎

Transits and eclipses of the satellites by Jupiter have been of great importance to physics and astronomy. In 1675, the Danish astronomer Olaus Roemer prepared predictions of future eclipses and transits based upon the assumption of an infinite speed of light, when Earth and Jupiter were near their closest approach. Months later, when the distance between the two planets had lengthened, Roemer measured the errors in his predictions and was thereby able to come up with a fairly accurate estimate for the speed of light.

Except on the rare nights when Mars is closest to Earth and at its brightest, the only planetary or stellar object brighter than Jupiter is Venus. Because Jupiter requires 12 years to complete one revolution of the Sun, it is continuously visible in the night sky for periods measured in months. Observation of the Galilean moons, Great Red Spot, and cloud bands of this giant world, are excellent activities for any urban observer.

Saturn

If Jupiter is the monarch of the Solar System, beautiful Saturn is a pretender to the throne. With a mass of 95 earths, this ringed world is a beautiful sight in binoculars or a small telescope. Although the famous rings of Saturn are around 70,000 miles across, their thickness is probably measured in miles or less. We know this because the rings, which coincide with the planet's equator, are inclined at 27 degrees to the plane of the orbit.

SATURN ACTIVITY 1

Sketching the Rings

The aspect of Saturn's rings will vary periodically. When viewed edge-on, they sometimes seem to vanish in the telescope's eyepiece. By sketching the appearance of the rings during the months when Saturn is continuously visible in the night sky, and by repeating this over a period of a few years, you will develop a record of the changing aspect of this planet's rings.

With a 3-inch aperture telescope, Cassini's division can be observed. This 3,000-mile-wide gap is the darkest feature of the ring system and may consist of an actual break in the rings. If your telescope is equipped with a reticle eyepiece, one telescopic activity is the measurement of the angular extent of the rings and their separation from the planet.

Voyager photographs reveal a great deal of fine structure in Saturn's rings. Small satellites called *shepherd moons* may gravitationally herd the ice and dust particles in the ring systems of all the gas giants. The rings themselves may be remnants of comets, asteroids, or moonlets that long ago approached the gas giant worlds too closely.

Like Jupiter, Saturn has latitudinal cloud bands that are most likely due to methane, ammonia, and other "impurities" in a prevailing hydrogen/helium atmosphere. Saturn's cloud bands, however, are more diffuse than those of Jupiter and are harder to observe. (You might experiment with various colored filters to see whether any of them help resolve the cloud bands from your location.) Near the equator, the rotational rate of Saturn's cloudtops is slightly more than 10 hours. At latitude 60 degrees, the rotation rate is close to 11 hours.

SATURN ACTIVITY 2

Viewing the Planet's Large Satellites

As well as its magnificent ring system, Saturn is blessed with a wide array of satellite attendants. Titan, which is about the same size as Mercury (4,800 km in diameter) and has a dense methane atmosphere, can be viewed through a 2-inch telescope during ideal conditions. Rhea can be seen with a 3-inch diameter instrument. Dione, Tethys, and Iapetus are visible in a 5-inch telescope. While you may have only a little luck in viewing Saturn's satellites from an urban setting such as New York, urban astronomers blessed with relatively clear skies, such as those in cities of the American Southwest, will do somewhat better. ■

Saturn is almost 10 times as far from the Sun as is Earth. This cold and distant planet circles the Sun once every 29.5 years.

Of all the naked-eye planets, Saturn moves the slowest through the sky. It can therefore be observed in the night sky for months on end. At maximum light, its visual apparent magnitude is −0.4. Only one star in the northern sky, Sirius, is brighter.

Beyond Saturn

Beyond Saturn are the planets Uranus, Neptune, and Pluto. Although Uranus is just visible to the naked eye, these outer planets are not dramatic targets for urban observers. Unless you are fortunate enough to have a sufficiently large telescope, ideal viewing conditions, and a great deal of patience, you will most likely confine your planet observing to Venus, Mars, Jupiter, and Saturn.

CHAPTER 6

Unusual Stars

I open the scuttle at night and see the far-sprinkled
    systems,
And all I see multiplied as high as I can cipher
    edge but the rim of the farther systems

Wider and wider they spread, expanding, always
    expanding,
Outward and outward and forever outward.
    —Walt Whitman, *Song of Myself* (1881)

Whether you look at the night sky with the naked eye, with binoculars, or with a telescope, you will probably concentrate at first upon the Moon, the naked-eye planets, and the constellations. Even under high magnification and through a wide-aperture telescope, the stars are still distant points of light. To see a sunlike disk of even a very large and relatively near star, you need one of the world's largest telescopes and sophisticated computer techniques to compensate for the vagaries of Earth's atmosphere.

As well as appearing visually different from planets and satellites, stars are physically very different. Unlike planets and satellites, which shine by reflected light, stars generate their own light by thermonuclear fusion. The least massive star is 80 times or so as massive as Jupiter, the most massive planet in our Solar System.

Through a good set of binoculars or a small telescope, the stars do seem brighter and there are more of them. Many amateur observers give up quickly on stellar observing simply because of the huge numbers of stars from which to choose. With the naked eye, a few thousand stars are visible on a clear night in an ideal location. In even a small telescope, the membership in the visible stellar host runs into the millions.

STELLAR OBSERVING ACTIVITY 1

Star Counts

One observing activity that can easily be performed by the novice star observer is to estimate the number of stars that are observed in the field of view of the instrument when he or she looks in a particular direction in the sky and to compare this estimate with what the naked eye can see. From an urban location in the Northern Hemisphere, only a few hundred stars will be visible with the naked eye, and the limiting visual apparent magnitude will be about 4. With binoculars or a 2-inch diameter telescope, a few thousand stars brighter than visual magnitude 8 or so will be visible. With a larger instrument—say, 4 to 6 inches—you should be able to image very many more stars (some as dim as magnitude 10) even through urban skies. ∎

Amid the plethora of distant suns are some jewels, especially the brilliantly colored multiple stars. Some of these are collected into enormous clusters or galaxies that are visible to the naked eye and are a treat under even very low magnification.

There are a few hundred billion stars in our Milky Way Galaxy. Astronomers estimate that the visible universe contains additional billions of galaxies. This chapter concentrates upon only a few of the prettiest and most fascinating galactic and extragalactic objects. All are visible to the naked eye or through a small instrument. Before individual sky objects are considered, some discussion of star colors and evolution is in order.

Star Colors and Evolution

Most stars in the night sky seem to be white or yellow to the typical human observer. But look to the constellation Orion. The bright star Rigel denotes the Hunter's right foot (from the perspective of the observer). Betelgeuse is in his left shoulder, just below his upraised shield. On a clear night in a fairly dark location, the naked eye is sufficient to denote the color difference between these two stars. Rigel shines with a bluish tint and is classified as a blue giant star. The orange Betelgeuse is classified as a red giant. (If you refer to the Hertzsprung–Russell diagram in Appendix 7, you will see that star surface temperature has much to do with color. Blue stars are considerably hotter than yellow or red stars.)

Between these two stars in one constellation, more is spanned than the visible spectrum. Rigel (a comparative youngster) is almost 60,000 times as luminous as the Sun and is 50 times more massive than the Sun. Someday, Rigel may explode as a supernova and temporarily outshine all the stars in the Milky Way Galaxy combined! Our yellow Sun glows with a surface temperature of about 6,000 degrees Celsius. Extravagant Rigel is considerably hotter, with a surface temperature in the vicinity of 20,000 degrees Celsius.

Betelgeuse is cooler than our Sun, with a surface temperature of about 3,000 degrees Celsius. If the Sun were replaced by Betelgeuse, the tenuous outer atmosphere of this red giant would extend beyond the orbit of Mars. When the Sun someday evolves to the red giant stage, it will become a very large and luminous, cool, red star, the inner planets of Mercury, Venus, and most likely Earth will be engulfed by the expanded Sun. But you have no cause to worry—the Sun should be stable for another 5,000 million years or so!

Although Betelgeuse and Rigel in the constellation Orion are among the brightest stars in the sky, they are certainly not among the nearest. Both are around 1,400 light-years from the Sun. The light-year, a basic unit of stellar astronomy, is the distance traversed by light moving at 186,300 miles per second in one year. (For those who like distance comparisons, one light-year is identical to 63,240 astronomical units.)

Most stars in the universe are far more modest than Betelgeuse and Rigel. Cool red dwarfs (small, cool, comparatively dim stars) will last for trillions of years; Rigel will exhaust its fusion fuel in tens of millions. We have some indication that either Rigel or Betelgeuse or both have evolved significantly in the last few thousand years. Greek astronomers classified Betelgeuse as Alpha Orionis, the brightest star in the constellation Orion, and Rigel as Beta Orionis, the second brightest. Today, Rigel is almost half a magnitude brighter.

It is known that the trained human eye can judge stellar magnitudes to an accuracy of about 0.1 or 0.2 magnitude. (More about this later!) It seems unlikely that the ancient Greek astronomers would be in error by almost 0.5 magnitude; it is much more likely that one or both of these brilliant but unstable stars have changed dramatically during the last few thousand years.

Stellar evolution can best be understood by referring to a Hertzsrpung–Russell (H–R) diagram such as the one in Appendix 7. This chart, which was developed just before World War I by Ejnar Hertzsrpung of Denmark and Henry Norris Russell of the United States, allows astronomers to classify surface temperatures, colors, and luminosities of all stars on the same diagram. The simple classification scheme of the H–R diagram belies the incredible labors that a number of women astronomers at American observatories spent in their analysis of photographs of the spectra of many thousands of stars.

During most of its life, a star is a "main-sequence dwarf." Such stable hydrogen-burners, like the Sun, fall on or near the line on the H–R diagram called the *main sequence*. Main-sequence dwarf stars are maintained in near-equilibrium during their long period of stability. Gravity, which tends to make the star collapse, is exactly balanced by the pressure of the emitted electromagnetic radiation, which makes the star expand.

Main-sequence stars are classified in a number of spectral classes (O, B, A, F, G, K, M, R, N, S) of decreasing surface temperature. Hot O- and B-class stars are blue and short lived; red M-class stars are smaller, dimmer, cooler, and much longer lived. Astronomy students have long remembered the spectral sequence by using the mnemonic device "Oh, Be A Fine Girl (or Guy), Kiss Me Right Now Sweetheart." Experienced urban astronomers will be able to roughly classify the stars they observe by the predominant star color.

When a star begins to contract from an interstellar gas and dust cloud or nebula, it enters the H–R diagram from the upper right. As it begins to shine, most of the light results, not from nuclear fusion, but from friction as dust and gas falls onto its surface. Later, as temperatures and pressures build up near the star's core, fusion fires ignite. These thermonuclear reactions convert hydrogen in the star into helium and energy and are similar to the processes used in the hydrogen bomb and our primitive fusion reactors. The total amount of time for a star to condense from the primeval dust cloud to the main sequence is probably less than 100 million years.

A G-class star like our Sun remains on the main sequence for about 10,000 million years. At the conclusion of the Sun's existence, it will cool as it expands to the red giant stage. Most of the Sun's remaining fusion reserves will be squandered in 50 million years or so before it once again shrinks.

Instead of stopping at the main sequence, a dying star passes through this band. Its fusion fuel exhausted, the star contracts toward its ultimate fate—that of a *white dwarf*. On the H–R diagram, white dwarfs are hot blue-white objects of low luminosity.

It is hard to imagine a white dwarf. To picture such a stellar corpse, first realize that a star like the Sun is a very massive object—about 330,000 times as massive as Earth. The Sun is also a very large object—with a radius of almost half a million miles.

When a star's fusion fires are exhausted, the radiation pressure of starlight can no longer balance the attractive force of gravity. The star collapses until it is roughly the size of Earth's Moon!

During its long senescence as a white dwarf, the star shines dimly but hotly. The luminosity results from internal energy that is being radiated away from the extinct star. When all the internal energy is gone, an extinct black dwarf—the nonluminous cold cinder of a star—will take the place of the former luminary.

In the exceedingly dense interior of a white dwarf, electrons have been stripped from the nuclei of the atoms and these subatomic particles are pushed close together in what is called a *degenerate* gas. For stars more than 1.5 times as massive as the Sun, stellar collapse continues until a very massive atomic nucleus about 10 miles in diameter called a *neutron star* results. Stars more than about 50 times as massive as our Sun continue their collapse even further and may leave our universe as exotic black holes.

Neutron stars are observable by radio astronomers only in nebulae resulting from supernova explosions. Black holes, long predicted by theoreticians but unobserved, have been evidenced by sophisticated observatory and orbital telescopes.

107

Although white dwarfs are too dim to be observed directly using small telescopes, there are some in the vicinity of our Sun. The companion of Sirius, the brightest star in the sky, was the first white dwarf to be photographed. Sirius itself is a more prosaic blue-white A-class main-sequence dwarf and is somewhat more luminous than the Sun. Sirius is the brightest star in our sky because of its proximity, not because of its intrinsic luminosity. This star is only 8.6 light-years from our Solar System.

Sirius, the Sun, and most other stars in the solar neighborhood are second- or third-generation stars. In the time between the formation of our galaxy shortly after the creation of the universe (about 15,000 million years ago) and the birth of our Sun (about 5,000 billion years ago), many stars began to shine, evolved, and died in the Milky Way. Some of these "oldsters" are still around, shining as dim, long-lived red dwarfs.

These earlier generations of stars are deficient in elements more massive than helium. When they are compared to middle-aged stars like the Sun and younger stars. Most of the chemical elements necessary for the formation of solid planets, atmospheres, rocks, life, and telescopes were synthesized within the atmospheres of the more massive of the ancient stars as they exploded in titanic supernova explosions.

As a young star shrinks toward the main sequence and as an old star ends this stable phase of its existence, the stellar luminosity is not constant. The study of such variable stars is of great astrophysical significance and is an area to which the amateur observer can make a real contribution.

STELLAR OBSERVING ACTIVITY 2

Star Colors

Before you observe variable stars, you might wish to develop your skills at classifying bright nonvariable stars. A good activity would be to use a star chart or star wheel to locate the brightest visible stars in various constellations in the evening sky. Then, as you observe a bright star through your binoculars or telescope, write down your impressions of its color. Later on, you could estimate its spectral class and compare your estimate with its tabulated spectral class. For best results in this activity, select stars that are fairly high in the sky. This will minimize the affects of Earth's atmosphere upon a star's apparent color. Also, this activity will be more satisfying if you can find an urban observing site reasonably free of light pollution. ■

Variable Stars

Unlike most stars, the visual apparent magnitude of a variable star is not constant. Some variations in stellar brightness are caused when two stars of widely different brightnesses circle a common center of mass as a binary star and the plane of their orbital motion is such that one star can occasionally pass in front of, or eclipse, the other (from the point of view of a terrestrial astronomer). The most famous eclipsing binary is the "demon star" Algol in the constellation Perseus. (According to Richard Hinckley Allen, the designation "demon star" probably arose because Algol is in the head of the Gorgon that is being carried by Perseus, not because of the star's variation.) Typically a magnitude 2 star, Algol's brightness dips by about one magnitude at intervals of roughly 2 days and 20 hours. Observers in the Northern Hemisphere will find Algol high in the evening sky during the winter and high in the predawn sky during the autumn.

Other variable stars are those that have not yet reached or have departed from the main sequence. These stars vary in brightness as they pulsate.

One class of very luminous pulsating stars are the Cepheids. Of use to astrophysicists as intergalactic distance indicators, the brightest Cepheids are thousands of times more luminous than the Sun. They are classified as F or G supergiants. The class is named after Delta Cephei, the fourth brightest star in the constellation

Cepheus. This star, with a visual apparent magnitude that varies between 3.6 and 4.3, has a period of 5.4 days.

Fairly bright and easy to find even in murky suburban skies, Delta Cephei can be observed over the course of one or two periods. Its brightness can be estimated by comparing it visually to nearby stable stars in Cepheus. In an interesting experiment with this star, the teacher (in this case, the author) of a graduate astronomy lab at Wesleyan University had each member of a summer class observe this star and estimate its magnitude for as many clear nights as possible over a one-week interval. When the results were later collected and compared, almost all of the students agreed within 0.2 or 0.3 magnitude. Photographic and photoelectric photometry are of course more accurate, but the efficiency of the unaided human eye in estimating differential star brightness is certainly nothing to sneer at!

VARIABLE STAR ACTIVITY 1

Observing Delta Cephei

If you wish to observe Delta Cephei and monitor its changes in visual apparent magnitude, you should start by using the star charts in Appendix 6 or a star wheel to familiarize yourself with the appearance of this constellation in the sky. Because Cepheus is a circumpolar constellation, it is always above the horizon in the mid-latitude Northern Hemisphere.

Then, you could use the appropriate finding chart in Figure 6–1 to locate Delta Cephei. Next, you should compare the brightness of this star to some of its neighbors each night for about one week. The approximate visual apparent magnitudes of some of the other stars in Cepheus are included in the finding chart. Although you can use binoculars or a telescope for this activity, the unaided eye yields excellent results.

From an urban site, you should observe Delta Cephei when the constellation Cepheus is highest in the northern evening sky. The

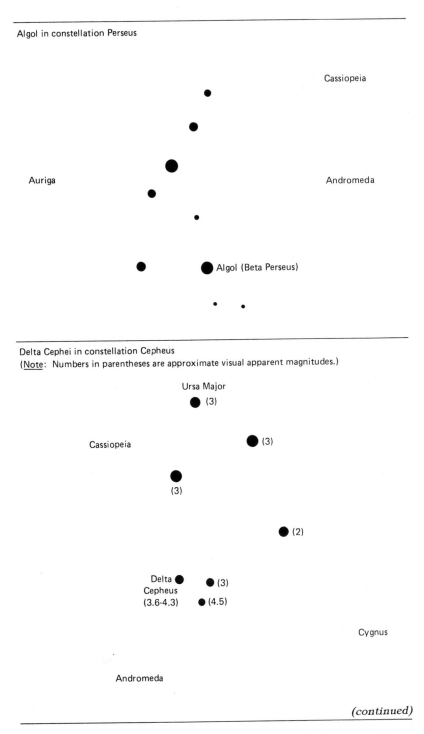

Algol in constellation Perseus

Cassiopeia

Auriga

Andromeda

Algol (Beta Perseus)

Delta Cephei in constellation Cepheus
(<u>Note</u>: Numbers in parentheses are approximate visual apparent magnitudes.)

Ursa Major
● (3)

Cassiopeia
● (3)

● (3)

● (2)

Delta ● ● (3)
Cepheus
(3.6-4.3) ● (4.5)

Cygnus

Andromeda

(continued)

Figure 6-1 Finding charts for some common variable stars (charts aligned with north at top) (Adapted from J. Sanford, *Observing the Constellations*).

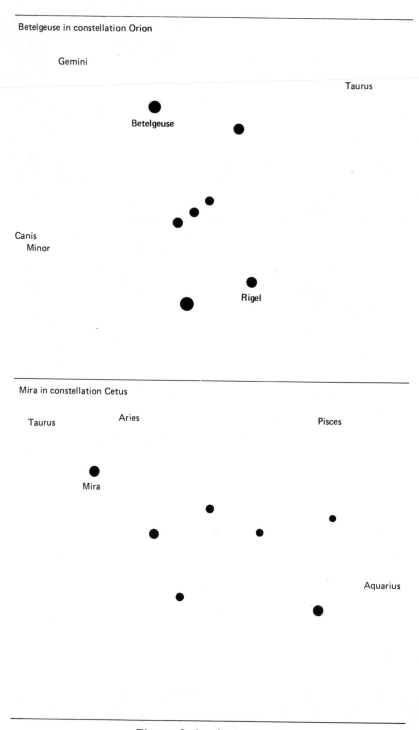

Betelgeuse in constellation Orion

Gemini

Taurus

Betelgeuse

Canis
Minor

Rigel

Mira in constellation Cetus

Taurus   Aries   Pisces

Mira

Aquarius

Figure 6–1   (continued)

best times of year for this activity are late summer, autumn, and early winter. ∎

Another Cepheid variable is none other than our North Star, Polaris. Also known as Alpha Ursa Minor, this F-class star varies by two-tenths of a magnitude during a period of just under four days.

In 1987, Nadine Dinshaw performed a student project using a 16-inch aperture telescope at the University of British Columbia. She recorded 237 spectrophotographs of Polaris, the North Star, over a seven-month period.

Polaris is a supergiant located 500 to 800 light-years from the Solar System. This star is a Cepheid variable, with a smaller, invisible companion. It varies in visual apparent magnitude between 2.6 and 2.8 during its four-day cycle, and its spectral class varies between F7 and F9. Spectral classes are divided in tenths: F0 is the hottest and brightest F star classification; F9 is the coolest and dimmest.

Analysis of Dinshaw's data by herself and by other observatory staffers revealed that the variation of Polaris may be slowing down and fading away. Within 10 to 20 years, Polaris may leave the variable phase of its evolutionary track. This is interesting because the Cepheid variable phase for a star as massive as Polaris has a duration in the neighborhood of 40,000 years. Astronomers should monitor this star closely to learn what comes next!

In the constellation Cetus, you can sometimes observe with the naked eye the marvelous long-period variable star Mira. Also known as Omicron Ceti, Mira usually is invisible to the naked eye, with a visual apparent magnitude of 8 to 10. At intervals of every 11 months or so, Mira will brighten to a visual apparent magnitude of 2.5 or even lower. The spectral class of this red supergiant is also slightly variable, which indicates that its surface temperature is not constant during the oscillation period. Located more than 200 light-years from Earth, Mira's radius changes by 20 percent during each cycle. The physical size of this star is, on the average, more than 400 times greater than that of our Sun.

VARIABLE STAR ACTIVITY 2

Observing Mira

You can perform a naked-eye observing activity using Mira if you are willing to continue for about a year. By utilizing Figure 6–1 and the star charts in Appendix 6 or a star wheel, you would locate Cetus in the sky and sketch the appearance of this constellation. Periodically, Mira will be visible in your nightly sketch. Of course, if you lack the patience and devotion for a one-year activity, you could consult the pages of *Sky & Telescope,* which publishes a monthly listing for observers of variable stars. ∎

Some of the long-period variables have semiregular periods. Notable among these is Betelgeuse in Orion, which varies between visual apparent magnitude 0.4 and 1.2. A few thousand semiregular variables are known in our galaxy. Oscillation periods for stars in this class are not dependable and typically vary between 30 and 2,000 days.

There are thousands of variable stars of these and other classes in our galaxy and others. The five selected for description here are those most easily found using the naked eye or a small telescope. Appendix 10 gives further information on some other easily observable variable stars.

If you wish to make a contribution to stellar and galactic astronomy but avoid arcane mathematics and expensive equipment, variable star observation might be for you. Naked-eye magnitude estimates are valuable, as are photographic and photometric measurements. One clearing house for variable star observation is the American Association of Variable Star Observers (AAVSO), which is located at 25 Birch Street, Cambridge, Massachusetts.

Binary Stars

The Sun, a single star, is definitely in the minority. Perhaps as many as two-thirds or three-quarters of the few hundred billion stars in our galaxy are binaries or multiples. If two or more stars are gravitationally associated with each other, they tend to revolve around a common center of mass. Long observation of the relative motions of members of a stellar binary is often required to confirm a gravitational bond; decades or centuries often are required for a complete revolution.

If there are more than two stars in the group, we usually find them arranged in pairs. Castor, the brightest star in Gemini, is a case in point. Observed through a 3- or 4-inch aperture telescope, this second magnitude star is resolved into two white components—with apparent visual magnitudes 2.7 and 3.7. These two orbit each other fairly quickly, within a period of about 350 years. Within an observer's lifetime, changes in the relative positions of the two components will be noticeable. The British astronomer William Herschel is credited with first noticing the relative motions of the two Castor components, in about 1804.

A third star, itself consisting of a pair of faint red dwarfs, circles the brighter Castor components in an orbit requiring roughly 10,000 years. Both of the brighter Castor components are themselves close doubles, but these can only be resolved spectroscopically. Castor is approximately 45 light years from the Sun.

Astronomers recognize four classes of double stars. Optical doubles are not truly connected in a gravitational sense. They seem close together to the terrestrial observer because of geometrical projection, but may actually be separated by hundreds of light-years.

BINARY STAR ACTIVITY 1

Observing Mizar and Alcor

Visual binaries are those stars that can be resolved by the human eye. Finding charts for some visual binaries are included in Figure 6–2. In almost all cases, binoculars or telescopes are required to resolve the components of a visual binary. A notable exception is the pair Mizar/Alcor, which is visible as the second star in the handle of the Big Dipper (Zeta Ursae Majoris). Mizar is the brighter of the two

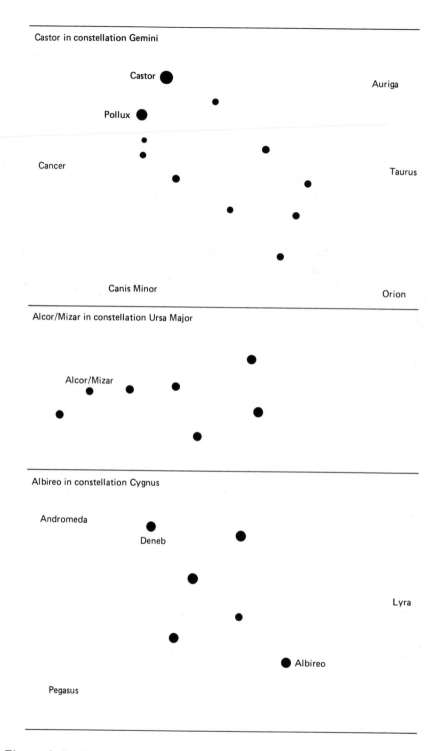

Figure 6–2 Finding charts for some common multiple stars (charts aligned with north at top) (Adapted from J. Sanford, *Observing the Constellations*)

with a magnitude of 2.4; Alcor's visual apparent magnitude is 4; and both members of this pair are white. During the past 1,000 years, Alcor may have brightened a bit. It was formerly used as an eyesight test by American Indians and various European armies. Today, even through murky urban skies, many observers can spot Alcor without the use of telescopes or binoculars.

Alcor and Mizar are approximately 88 light-years from the Sun. Each of the visible members are themselves *spectroscopic* binaries. This class of binary stars is characterized by pairs that are so close that no telescope can resolve them. Their binary nature is determined by observing shifts in spectral emission and absorption lines. ■

Astrometric binaries, the remaining class of binary stars, are perhaps the most exciting. Unfortunately, *astrometric* binaries cannot be directly observed. In an astrometric binary, a nonluminous or subluminous object revolves around a much brighter star. By observing the proper motion of the visible member of the pair across the star field—a process that may take decades of observation—the presence of the dim object can be deduced by analyzing positional perturbations. Astronomers specializing in the discipline of astrometry have uncovered indirect evidence of subluminous stars, brown dwarfs (objects intermediate in size between stars and planets), and even planets of Jupiter's size or larger circling nearby stars.

BINARY STAR ACTIVITY 2

Observing Various Doubles

Appendix 11 presents information on some selected binaries that can be observed using binoculars or a small telescope. Notable among these are Beta Cygni (also known as Albireo). With a magnitude of 3.2, the orange, brighter component contrasts nicely with its blue, 5.4 magnitude companion. In observing a close pair, the human eye sometimes accentuates color differences. Some of the colorful descriptions in nineteenth-century handbooks—"topaz, garnet, pale violet"—are more a result of this subjective effect than of objective star colors.

When you are observing doubles, it is wise to choose a park or beach observing site since heat rising from driveways or pavement will cause the seeing conditions to deteriorate. You should allow plenty of time—at least half an hour—for your telescope to reach the same temperature as the environment. (This will be sufficient time for all the metal and glass components in the telescope to expand or contract with the temperature.) Also, you should dress warmly and keep your body, as much as possible, out of the light path. Differential atmospheric heating will produce turbulence that could ruin your observation session.

If you have a reticle eyepiece for your telescope, you might wish to observe the relative positions and angular separation of the components of your favorite binaries over the years. If you are patient and careful, you may be able to detect orbital motion for some close pairs. ■

Many stars can also be found in galactic star clusters and in other galaxies. Although billions of galactic and extragalactic nebulae are known to astronomers, only a few of these "deep-sky" objects are easily observable from an urban setting.

Deep-Sky Objects

A number of different varieties of deep-sky objects can be observed with a small telescope or binoculars. A few of these are visible to the naked eye. Finding charts for some deep-sky objects are included in Figure 6–3.

Most of these objects are referred to by their "M-number," after Charles Messier, a French astronomer who began cataloging them in the late eighteenth century. Paradoxically, Messier was not investigating these objects because of their then unknown astrophysical significance. He was instead interested in locating cloudlike celestial objects that could be mistaken for comets by less-than-experienced sky observers.

One of the most favored of the Messier objects is M31, the Great Spiral Nebula in Andromeda. With a visual apparent magnitude of 4.8, this spiral galaxy can easily be seen from any moderately dark location whenever Andromeda is in the sky.

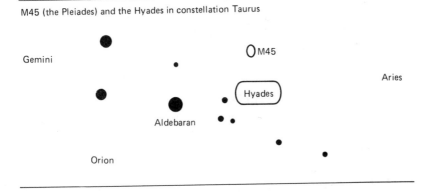

M31, the Great Spiral Galaxy in constellation **Andromeda**

M31

Andromeda

Pegasus

M42, the Great Nebula in constellation Orion

M42

M45 (the Pleiades) and the Hyades in constellation Taurus

Gemini

M45

Aries

Hyades

Aldebaran

Orion

Figure 6–3 Finding charts for some common deep-sky objects (charts aligned with north at top) (Adapted from J. Sanford, *Observing the Constellations*)

119

The first known observations of the Great Spiral Nebula were made around A.D. 900. The Arab astronomer Al-Sufi mentioned it as a "little cloud" in his *Book of the Fixed Stars,* which was first published in A.D. 964.

To the naked eye, M31 does not appear to be a virtual twin of the Milky Way Galaxy as it does in long-exposure observatory photographs. Instead, it does indeed resemble a little cloud. Even with telescopes as large as 20 inches in aperture under fine seeing conditions, the eye does not capture the detail of the photographic plate.

Even though it is somewhat disappointing to view, the Great Spiral Nebula is superlative to discuss. It contains hundreds of billions of stars, is more than two million light-years distant from the Milky Way Galaxy, and is the most observed extragalactic object. The Great Spiral Nebula in Andromeda is somewhat larger than the Milky Way Galaxy, which has a diameter of around 100,000 light-years.

The Great Spiral Nebula is attended by two companion dwarf elliptical galaxies. One of these, M32, has a visual apparent magnitude of 8.7 and can be viewed in a small telescope about one degree southwest of the Great Spiral Nebula.

DEEP-SKY ACTIVITY 1

Observing the Great Spiral Nebula in Andromeda

You will easily locate this spiral galaxy from a moderately dark urban location during clear autumn evenings. Then, the constellation Andromeda is fairly close to the zenith (overhead point).

To the naked eye, M31 seems to be a hazy, small cloudlike patch in the clear autumn sky. In binoculars or a small telescope, the Great Spiral Nebula seems like a featureless, bright oval. To observe the true extent of this object, use low telescope power and as large a field of view as possible.

In 1885, the first supernova ever observed in a galaxy outside our own was discovered in M31. Such an event should occur about once every century in a typical spiral galaxy. If you regularly observe and sketch M31 and look for variations in its brightness, perhaps you will be the lucky observer to first spot the next stellar explosion in that galaxy! ■

Our own galaxy has two companions. These small irregular galaxies, the Magellanic Clouds, can be viewed only from the Southern Hemisphere.

Although M31 is somewhat of a disappointment to most amateur observers, it is more than compensated for by the beautiful blue-green M42, the Great Nebula in Orion.

Messier 42 is a galactic object, at a distance of around 1,500 light-years. With a visual apparent magnitude of 4.2, it has been known throughout recorded history as a star in Orion's sword. Its cloudlike or nebulous appearance was first noted by Nicholas Peiresc in 1610, about a year after Galileo first pointed his telescope skyward. Messier 42 and the constellation Orion are best viewed during winter evenings.

This nebula is actually a star nursery. New stars, some less than a few million years old, are illuminating this cloud of interstellar dust and gas from within. Some of these young stars have been observed to vary irregularly in luminosity as they shrink slowly toward the main sequence.

In almost any instrument, the Orion nebula is a dramatic sight. Although most observers will see this object as a brilliant blue-green, reddish filaments stand out in high-quality color photographs because the spectral sensitivity of the human eye differs somewhat from that of the photographic emulsion.

DEEP-SKY ACTIVITY 2

Observing the Orion Nebula

The constellation Orion is easily observed from an urban site during late autumn and early winter evenings when it is high in the eastern sky and in late winter and early spring evenings when it is high in the west. This constellation is highest in the sky, somewhat south of the zenith, on midwinter evenings.

You will soon learn to recognize Orion the Hunter by the three stars in the hunter's belt. To find the Great Nebula M42, move south from the central belt star along the Hunter's sword.

For beautiful views of the entire Orion nebula, use binoculars or a telescope eyepiece with low magnification and high field of view. Higher magnification will show more detail and stars in this nebula's central region. ∎

Around five billion years ago, our Sun must have formed in a stellar association much like M42. Later, as the stars ignited and began to blow off much of the remnant gas and dust, the nebula in which the Sun formed may have resembled M45, the Pleiades.

Located in the constellation Taurus, this open cluster has a visual apparent magnitude of 1.6 and is around 400 light-years from the Sun. Although known in ancient times as "the Seven Sisters" or "the Seven Virgins," only six of these stars are clearly visible to the unaided eye. Once again, some of these young stars may have altered their luminous output in the last few thousand years.

Homer's *Odyssey* contains sailing instructions from the Island of Calypso that refer to the Pleiades. To ancient Mediterranean seafarers, this arrangement of stars may have been as significant as "the Plough" (known to us as the Big Dipper).

As the aperture of the viewing instrument increases, the visible number of stars associated with the Pleiades also increases. Several hundred young, white stars are members of this cluster; most of them are contained in a sphere 50 light-years or so in diameter. Some of the nebulosity in the Pleiades can be observed in photographs. It is believed that most of the nebulosity is due to microscopic solid particles that have not yet been absorbed in infant solar systems or ejected from the cluster by radiation pressure.

DEEP-SKY ACTIVITY 3

Observing the Pleiades

To locate the Pleiades, first refer to the appropriate finding chart in Figure 6–3. From Orion's belt, trace an imaginary line northwest. The first bright star you come to will be Aldebaran in the constellation Taurus. Continue following the line beyond Aldebaran. This star is about equidistant between the Orion belt stars and the Pleiades.

On winter evenings, M45 (the Pleiades) is highest in the sky. In the early spring shortly after sundown, you will find this cluster about midway between the zenith and the horizon in the western sky.

A pair of binoculars or a wide-field Newtonian reflector is the best instrument for observing this cluster. If you are fortunate enough to observe on a night when the urban sky is unusually transparent, you may be able to glimpse some of the nebulosity still associated with M45. ∎

Besides the Pleiades, in Taurus you can also observe the looser and older galactic cluster, the Hyades. Around 130 light-years distant from our Solar System, the Hyades cluster is approximately 400 million years old.

Beyond the disk of our spiral galaxy is a halo of tight globular clusters. One of these, M13 in Hercules, is barely visible to the naked eye, with a visual apparent magnitude of 5.7. Messier 13 is approximately 23,000 light-years from the Sun.

The 100,000 or so stars in this cluster are much older than the Sun. Many of the stars in M13 can be observed in a 4-inch aperture telescope. Direct observation will actually yield better resolution of the central portion of this globular cluster than photographs because of overexposure.

A number of other deep-sky objects are visible to the naked eye in the Northern Hemisphere and can be most rewarding to the observer equipped with binoculars or a telescope. Of particular note is Praesepe the Beehive. With a magnitude of 3.7, this open cluster in Cancer is often compared with the Pleiades or the Hyades. Praesepe is more open than the Pleiades and contains many orange or yellow stars. Roughly halfway between Regulus in Leo and Pollux in Gemini, the lavish collection of stars comprising the Beehive is best observed using binoculars.

Additional stellar collections can be observed by pointing your binoculars or telescope toward the Milky Way. At least one Milky Way star cloud has an M-number because it is detached from the rest of the Milky Way. This is M24, an object of 4.5 magnitude in Sagittarius. Also in Sagittarius, invisible behind the many lanes of faint stars, dust, and gas that comprise the spiral arms of our galaxy, is the galactic center. A black hole as massive as a few hundred or thousand Suns may lurk in the center of the Milky Way Galaxy.

Although most of us take it quite for granted, there is one stellar object of great significance quite nearby (in galactic terms). Best of all, we need not go out late at night to observe this celestial body, which is, of course, the nearest star to Earth—our Sun.

CHAPTER 7

To View the Sun— and the Dragon That Stalks It

For envied Wit, like Sol eclipsed, makes known
Th'opposing body's grossness, not its own.
When first that sun too powerful beams displays,
It draws up vapors which obscures its rays;
But even those clouds at last adorn its way.
Reflect new glories and augment the day.
—Alexander Pope, *Essay on Criticism Part II* (1711)

Our Sun, that enormous, brilliant ball of gases that dominates our Solar System, is a fascinating and vivid target for observation. Perhaps because the Sun is so vital to all life on Earth, people are easily drawn to a sunwatch session.

For example, on a beautiful early summer Sunday morning when members of the Amateur Astronomers Association of New York (and the author) assembled a solar observatory at the entrance to the Central Park Zoo in Manhattan, people began to gather.

They watched with interest as the members unpacked the telescope, tripod, and associated equipment. Periodically, one of the astronomers would talk to the crowd and let them know that solar observing would commence very soon. The dynamics of crowd behavior was quite marvelous: One minute, no one was there; then, one interested bystander attracted a few others; soon, there were dozens of people waiting for the completion of the assembly task.

Seeing a gathering crowd, a free-lance juggler unpacked his gear not 20 feet from the observing site. For the balance of the afternoon, people shuttled between the two events. Skateboarders, bicyclists, strollers, and zoo-goers lined up for their chance to view the Sun. Between 1 and 3 P.M. a few hundred people or more viewed the Sun.

For these amateur astronomers (as well as the author), the successful sunwatch was the culmination of months of planning. The first item needed was an appropriate telescope. An 8-inch aperture Schmidt–Cassegrain reflector equipped with a clock drive was finally obtained. A neutral-density filter was also obtained. Fitting snugly over the telescope aperture, this filter reduced sunlight intensity to a safe and comfortable level. White-light filters like the one used in this sunwatch reduce the intensity of all sunlight colors as equally as possible. In most cases, such filters act by absorption, 99.99 percent of ultraviolet, blue, yellow, red, and infrared sunlight is absorbed, and only about 0.01 percent of these colors passes through the optical system to the eyepiece.

One requirement for the observing site was electricity for the clock drive. Although clock-drive battery packs are commercially available, a site with available electrical outlets greatly simplifies the preparation process. In this case, an information kiosk near the entrance to the Central Park Zoo had the desired outlets. This site, near 63rd Street and Fifth Avenue, proved to be ideal. No tall buildings or towering trees were nearby; the group had good coverage of the Sun from the spring through the autumn, the ideal times for viewing our parent star from a location in New York City.

Through a 3- to 8-inch aperture telescope, which is equipped with a clock drive to follow celestial objects and with a sufficiently strong neutral-density filter, the Sun is a dramatic object. *Never, never observe the Sun through a telescope without a good filter.* For eye safety, make sure that the filter used is emplaced over the aperture of the telescope and that it reduces the intensity of incident sunlight by at least a factor of 10,000 times. (As discussed later in this chapter, projection of the filtered solar image is a safe alternative to direct viewing through the eyepiece.) The photosphere is clearly visible as are sunspots on the Sun's visible surface. Sunspots, temporary regions of slightly lower temperature on the photosphere, tend to cluster in groups and may predominate in one hemisphere. Through clear urban skies and a telescope equipped with a white-light filter, you will be able to observe that the Sun's brightness falls off toward the limb. This phenomenon can be explained by the fact that most of the Sun's energy is produced near its core.

SOLAR ACTIVITY 1
The Naked-Eye Sun

One naked-eye solar activity that is quite simple but yet elegant is the construction of a simple sundial. (The author first learned of this activity from Professor Emeritus Esther Sparberg of Hofstra University, Long Island, New York.) You could construct a personal sundial equipped with a central vertical shaft, or gnomon, by using easily available material. The length and position of the Sun's shadow is monitored periodically, thereby allowing you to observe the seasonal variation of the Sun's angle and daylight duration. This can also be an excellent application of high school trigonometry. (The length of the Sun's shadow will be inversely related to the Sun's altitude above the horizon.)

For best results, you should mount your central shaft (which can be as simple as a pencil or as elaborate as a sculpted obelisk) in the center of a circle that has the cardinal points of the compass (north, northeast, east, southeast, south, southwest, west, and northwest) labeled. This circle is the horizontal base for your sundial and can be constructed of wood, cardboard, or any other suitable material. The direction of the Sun's shadow and its length can therefore be readily monitored whenever the Sun is in the sky. Try to keep track of the Sun's position at a constant time—say, noon—from one season to the next. ■

Our Sun—The Closest Star

From the galactic perspective, there is nothing particularly distinguished about our Sun. It is one of several hundred billion stars in the Milky Way Galaxy, which is itself only one of billions of galaxies in the universe. Not only is "Sol" (the Roman name for the Sun) not at the center of the universe, it is not even at the center of the Milky Way. We are located about halfway between the rim and the core of our galaxy.

The Sun is classified as a fairly typical spectral-class-G main-sequence dwarf. About five billion years ago, an interstellar nebula similar perhaps to Messier 42 in Orion began to condense. At some time previous to the initial condensation, atoms more massive than helium had drifted into this primeval collection of dust and gas. These atoms of oxygen, carbon, uranium, and so on, had themselves been produced in the nuclear factory of an exploding supernova star.

Condensation continued until most of the nebular material was concentrated in a small number of bodies. The central, most massive condensation became the Sun. Those bodies farther out evolved into planets and smaller Solar System objects.

Our Sun is about halfway through its 10-billion-year life as a main-sequence star. The core of the Sun is mostly helium. In a region around this core, temperatures and pressures are sufficient for thermonuclear processes to convert hydrogen into helium and energy.

Initially in the form of gamma rays, this released energy reacts with the dense matter near it. Gradually, as energy from the fusion fires proceeds outward by convection, it is converted into less energetic forms of electromagnetic energy. When it finally emerges at the Sun's visible surface, or photosphere, most of the energy is in the form of visible light. The Sun is a prodigious emitter, however, all across the electromagnetic spectrum—from gamma rays to radio waves.

Most of the mass of the Solar System is concentrated in the Sun, which is more than 300,000 times as massive as Earth. Even the most massive world in the Solar System, Jupiter, is a mere 1/1000 of the Sun's mass.

Its physical size also dwarfs the planets. The Sun's diameter is more than 100 times that of Earth and about 10 times that of Jupiter. The gas giant planets like Jupiter are actually much more sunlike than the inner worlds such as Earth. Like the Sun, Jupiter is mostly hydrogen and helium. Unlike the Sun, these worlds are simply not massive enough for the fusion fires to ignite near their cores.

As energy reaches the Sun's visible surface, or photosphere, the convection cells that have been carrying it up from the interior become visible. High-altitude photographs have revealed these cells as granulation on the solar surface. Typical granules are a few hundred miles across and last for less than 10 minutes. These are the tops of the convection cells, carrying solar energy outward. Careful observation of granulation from balloons and satellites has revealed the spectral signature of hot gases rising from the solar interior and cooler gases falling back. Solar magnetic fields seem to influence granule concentrations and are also significant in the evolution of sunspots—a form of solar activity that is easily observed from an urban site. Sunspots appear darker than the surrounding portions of the Sun through a neutral-density white-light filter because these temporary solar markings are 1,500 degrees Celsius cooler than the surrounding photosphere. Sunspots are still pretty warm, however, at a respectable 4,500 degrees Celsius or so.

SOLAR ACTIVITY 2

Observing Sunspots through a Telescope

To observe sunspots from an urban site, a telescope with a fairly small aperture will be ample. Although more detail will be visible through an 8-inch instrument, good results can be obtained with a 4-inch Schmidt–Cassegrain equipped with a clock drive and white-light filter. The filter used should generally cut incident sunlight by a factor of 10,000 times or more. *Never view the Sun with the unaided naked eye or through an unfiltered telescope.*

Before you view the Sun through the telescope–filter combination, you should first make certain that the lens of your instrument's spotting scope closest to the Sun is covered. This precaution will help protect your vision if you inadvertently glance through the spotting scope's eyepiece.

Use the shadow of the telescope cast by the Sun to determine when your instrument is pointed directly toward our star. The telescope's shadow will be smallest when it is pointed directly toward the Sun.

On a clear day from an urban viewing site, close examination of a sunspot through your telescope under low magnification will indicate that its structure is not uniform. A central dark region, called the *umbra,* is surrounded by a lighter region, called the *penumbra.* The magnetic field within a sunspot is considerably stronger than the magnetic field of the surrounding photosphere.

A possible sunspot observing activity is to sketch your view of the Sun's photosphere at intervals of a few days. If you identify and track recognizable groups of sunspots, you should be able to verify that the Sun's rotation rate at the equator is approximately 25 days and that its rotation rate at latitude 30 degrees is about 27.5 days.

The lifetime of a sunspot varies from hours to months. Your repeated observational sketches of sunspot groups may therefore contain variations caused by sunspot evolution. ∎

Near the limb of the Sun, the skilled observer can sometimes make out bright regions called *faculae* or *plages.* These regions might be bright parts of the Sun's lower atmosphere, or chromosphere, in the high magnetic fields associated with sunspots. Faculae are visible as localized bright regions on the solar disk through a telescope equipped with a white-light filter.

One reason for the strong influence of magnetic fields on the Sun's appearance is the physical state of the hydrogen, helium, and trace elements constituting the Sun. Because of the high temperature, a significant fraction of the atoms are ionized. The resulting electrically charged particles are strongly affected by magnetic fields.

If you utilize a different type of filter, a spectral-line filter, you can sometimes see apparent bridges of ionized gas, or plasma, rising high above the solar surface and then falling back. These prominences, which are best observed near the solar limb during periods of intense solar activity, tend to follow magnetic field lines during their spectacular trajectories. Some of the matter in these eruptions moves well into the Sun's upper atmospheric layer, or corona, at speeds as high as 800 miles per second!

A spectral-line filter, unlike a white-light filter, transmits only a narrow range of wavelengths or colors. One of the favorite spectral-line filters for both amateur and professional solar observers is the hydrogen-alpha filter.

In an H-alpha filter, the chromosphere becomes visible as a mottled red ball. Filaments are sometimes observed on the chromosphere. If the Sun's rotation period of 25 days (near the equator) takes one of the filaments toward the solar limb, the observant astronomer will learn to his or her delight that filaments viewed near the center of the Sun's visible disk are often seen as prominences near the solar limb.

During periods of intense solar activity, solar flares sometimes erupt. The visible aspect of a solar flare is the brightening of a sizable portion of the solar disk. Enormous quantities of energy are released across the electromagnetic spectrum. The stream of ionized particles constantly departing from the Sun into interplanetary space—the solar wind—becomes far more intense during a solar flare.

When the flare-amplified solar wind reaches the upper atmosphere of Earth, we are often treated to extensive auroral displays as these particles interact with atmospheric gases. Shortwave radio transmissions become less reliable as the reflecting layers in Earth's ionosphere are temporarily impaired.

Solar flares are not particularly common. Accurate flare prediction seems to be somewhat beyond current capabilities.

While solar flares do not seem to be a health hazard to those living at the bottom of Earth's ocean of air, radiation associated with them may affect crews and passengers on high-flying airliners. The supersonic Concorde, which operates at 60,000 feet or so in the stratosphere, may be the most vulnerable of commercial aircraft to solar flares. Most of the radiation-shielding power of Earth's atmosphere is in the lower and denser layers of the troposphere and tropopause.

To date, no space mission has been terminated by a solar flare. During periods of peak solar activity, however, astronauts can sometimes see the tracks of solar wind particles in their closed eyes (caused as high-energy, electrically charged particles ionize atoms in the retina). The high solar wind during periods of intense solar activity also increases the density of atmospheric gases at orbital heights and thereby limits the lifetimes of some spacecraft.

Solar activity is apparently correlated with the sunspot cycle.

During an 11-year cycle, the number of sunspots visible on the solar surface increases and decreases. (If certain magnetic effects are taken into account, the solar cycle is actually 22 years.) The 1989–1990 solar maximum was more intense than most.

SOLAR ACTIVITY 3

Monitoring the Sun's Activity

An interesting observational activity is to obtain a quantitative measure of solar activity by counting sunspots and sunspot groups. These can be counted through your telescope–filter combination.

A frequently used measure of solar activity is the sunspot number (N) defined by

$$N = k\,(10g + s)$$

where g is the number of groups and s is the number of sunspots. The quantity k is an observer-dependent weighting function. If you become proficient at counting sunspots and groups, you can determine your value of k by comparing your value of N (assuming $k = 1$) with the daily values of N published every month in *Sky & Telescope*. Figure 7–1 presents some solar features visible through small telescopes equipped with appropriate filters. The activity number for this solar disk (assuming $k = 1$) is 15. ■

The Solar Flare Patrol

If you routinely observe the Sun during periods of high solar activity with an instrument of 4-inch or larger aperture equipped with a hydrogen-alpha filter, you may be the first to note the telltale brightening of a small region of the chromosphere that presages a major solar flare.

Suspected flares should be reported to the Central Bureau for Astronomical Telegrams at the Harvard-Smithsonian Center for

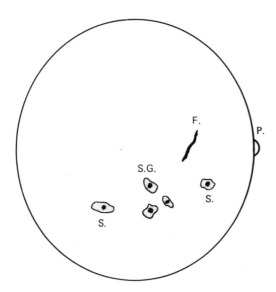

Figure 7-1 The Sun as seen through a small solar telescope (*Note:* In this inverted astronomical drawing, north is at the bottom. Objects labeled "S." are isolated sunspots; "S.G." is a sunspot group; "F." is a filament; and "P." is a prominence. The sunspots have been drawn with dark central umbras.)

Astrophysics in Cambridge, Massachusetts. You might also wish to report regular sunspot counts to the solar group of the American Association of Variable Star Observers (AAVSO), which is also in Cambridge.

But you should remember that a really intense solar flare may be a hazard to people above the protection of Earth's troposphere. Faxes or telephone calls to the local offices of Air France and British Airways might protect Concorde crews and passengers. Even though space programs are supplemented by extensive flare patrols, calls to the Johnson Space Flight Center in Houston, Texas, or the Soviet Embassy might give a little extra warning to space crews.

In conducting your systematic flare patrol, it would be a good idea to systemize data taking. You should observe the Sun on as many clear days as possible. Data should include date, time, a drawing of the solar disk with its sunspots, sunspot number, group number, and observer name.

Some Hints on Conducting a Sunwatch

The most important thing to remember about conducting a sunwatch is the potential danger of the Sun to the unprotected human eye. Unless the Sun is low in the sky or the sky is overcast, you should never glance at it with your unaided eye. Through any telescope, even through a small magnifying instrument such as a finder scope or binoculars, always make sure that a suitable white-light or spectral-line filter is in place before you attempt to observe the Sun.

Unfortunately, early telescopic astronomers were not aware of the potential danger of solar viewing. Galileo's eventual blindness was probably caused in part by his telescopic observations of the Sun in 1610. Modern observers need not repeat his experiment!

Some optical filters are designed to fit over the eyepiece of your instrument. To protect both your optics and your eyes, it is wiser instead to select filters that fit over the telescope aperture even though these are larger and generally more expensive.

It is not difficult to center your telescope's field of view upon the solar disk without glancing through the finder scope. Simply point the telescope tube approximately at the Sun and move it around until the tube's shadow is approximately circular.

If your telescope is properly aligned and is equipped with a clock drive, several techniques can be used to project the Sun's image. One is to use lightweight struts and white paper to construct a projection box so that the solar image can be projected outside of the eyepiece. A representation of such a device is shown in Figure 7–2.

One advanced solar experiment is to mount a small video camera at the eyepiece of a 4- to 8-inch diameter telescope equipped with a clock drive and appropriate solar filter. From your urban viewing station, you then could videotape the appearance of the Sun over a period of several hours.

According to Dr. Deborah Habor of the National Optical Solar Astronomy Observatory in Sunspot, New Mexico, such video data could be utilized by professional astronomers working in the new

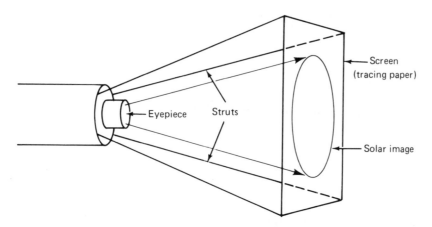

Figure 7-2 Use of a simple projection box to project an image of the solar disk from a telescope eyepiece.

discipline of helioseismology (a solar version of seismology, the study of earthquakes). The video data, obtained through a narrow bandpass filter such as the hydrogen-alpha spectral-line filter, would first be converted to a digitized format. An arcane mathematical technique called the *Fourier transform* would then be employed to reveal radial velocities of portions of the Sun's visible disk. Correlations among velocities of different parts of the solar disk provide knowledge of the "sunquakes." If you are interested in videotaping the Sun for such an application, you may wish to contact a local university to discuss the possibility of obtaining expert help in data reduction.

The Eclipse: Dragons in the Sky

From any urban location, particularly dramatic (although not everyday) celestial events are eclipses of the Sun and Moon. Many ancient people believed that eclipses were caused by celestial dragons. Today, we are much more knowledgeable regarding the cause of these events.

In a solar eclipse, the Moon passes between the observer and the Sun, and a bright day can momentarily be converted into night.

In the less dramatic but more common lunar eclipse, Earth passes between the Sun and Moon, and the full moon's color can darken for a period of hours to a crimson red.

Eclipses can be frustrating. You can plan for years, obtain the best of equipment, and perhaps travel for thousands of miles. Then, if it rains or is overcast, you are simply out of luck! To assist with your eclipse-observation planning, you may wish to consult the tables of dates and locations for lunar and solar eclipses that are given in Appendices 4 and 5.

Today, professional astronomers are less interested in solar eclipse observations than their counterparts were in previous generations. A host of sophisticated solar telescopes are located in ground-based and space-based observatories. Many are equipped with occulting "fingers" that can block out the Sun's disk to render its corona visible and can thus routinely record much of the data that could previously be recorded only during a total solar eclipse.

Prehistoric and Historic Eclipses

Before the dawn of written history, people must have watched the progress of solar and lunar eclipses with a mixture of fascination and terror. Some of these ancient impressions have come down to us in the form of the eclipse mythologies of many people. When the Sun's strength seemed to fail at the start of a total eclipse, some ancients danced while others resorted to self-mutilation or human sacrifice. When the dances and sacrifices failed and the Sun continued to weaken, faith in the constancy of the solar deity was shaken. Even in postpagan times, some incantations required to ward off the horrible eclipse still exist in religious practices. One is included in the Qur'an (or Koran), the holy book of Islam.

Although less dramatic than the solar eclipse, the lunar eclipse still inspired horror in the ancient world. Anglo-Saxon writings of the eighth century A.D. talk of a "horrible shield" covering the face of the Moon. In more ancient times, an Assyrian king petitioned the heavenly powers to protect his land from the evil foretold by a lunar eclipse.

Many ancient people developed colorful legends around the manner of beast that was attacking the Sun during a solar eclipse. In portions of the Orient, the Middle East, and medieval England, and among the Lapps, the creature was a dragon. Because both full and new lunar phases can be eclipsed, two dragons were required by some peoples in India.

Early Germans favored wolves as the sun-devouring critters. Dwellers in the East Indies blamed the fanciful griffin (a half eaglelike, half lionlike animal). Others believed that the main culprits were clouds, illness of the moon or sun god, efforts by these deities to better observe Earth, and nightmare monsters plunging earthward.

Some African tribes believed that the eclipse was a war between the Moon and Sun. Pacific and Australian aboriginal people favored the happier hypothesis that the Sun and Moon were making love during an eclipse. Even in civilized Greece, "the Cradle of Reason," many citizens believed that evil magicians were responsible for eclipses.

To restore the health of the celestial deities, the Canadian Tlingits would blow in unison toward the afflicted sky god. Japanese covered their wells and Eskimos upended their cooking pots to keep celestial poison from dripping in. Ancient Chinese danced to the tune of drums and gongs to drive off the eclipse dragon. A later Chinese invention, the firecracker, has been used by many modern folk to accomplish the same task. Guns and other weapons have been fired skyward in the twentieth century to scare the dragon(s).

At some time and location in the preliterate world, a ruling class of priests must have first realized that a great deal of power could be gained by developing means of predicting eclipses. At least 5,000 years ago, Megalithic "calendar wheels" such as Stonehenge in England had been constructed to keep track of the motions of the Sun and Moon. Although these people did not write and therefore left no permanent records of their convictions, we can be certain that they believed they were tracking deities, not celestial bodies.

In 1964, astronomer Gerald Hawkins used a digital computer to demonstrate that alignments of the Sun and Moon were almost certainly built into the design of Stonehenge. According to Hawkins and Sir Fred Hoyle, astronomer–priests could have monitored an 18.61-year eclipse cycle called the *Saros* by moving stakes around a circle of 56 chalk-filled holes surrounding Stonehenge. Since Stonehenge was in use for more than 1,000 years, there was plenty of time for a priesthood to have perfected its observations into a fairly accurate prediction scheme.

Although we can expect that later priesthoods such as the Chaldean astrologers (around 1000 B.C.) would have utilized the eclipse-prediction techniques pioneered in early Britain for their own advantage, most prescientific people were still horrified by the eclipse event. Perhaps the earliest written record of an eclipse is an 1136 B.C. lunar eclipse mentioned in an ancient Chinese book. According to folklore, two Chinese astronomers, Ho and Hsi, mispredicted an eclipse or failed to properly organize the archers, dancers, and musicians to drive off the dragon about 1,000 years earlier and thereby embarrassed the local ruler. These unfortunate astronomer–bureaucrats paid for their error with their lives.

Fortuitous eclipses have influenced world history. A 585 B.C. solar eclipse seems to have so upset the soldiers of Lydia and of Media that they declared a truce. This eclipse may therefore be one of the roots of the ancient Persian Empire. About 150 years later, an Athenian siege of Syracuse was similarly disrupted by a solar eclipse. Eclipse records are also found in the *Odyssey* of Homer, the Old Testament, and numerous Roman records.

In some ancient cases, the date of an eclipse was shifted to coincide with a significant terrestrial happening. This ploy was, unfortunately, not uncommon in medieval Europe. However, some good eclipse records from this period do exist, from both Christian and Islamic lands.

During the age of exploration, it was not uncommon for sophisticated European adventurers to use their knowledge of eclipse-prediction techniques to their own advantage. In 1504, Columbus convinced recalcitrant natives of Jamaica to reprovision his fleet by threatening not to restore the Moon during a total lunar eclipse. Many others—explorers, missionaries, and native leaders alike—used almanac predictions of eclipses for political and social purposes in the centuries that followed.

Eclipse Expeditions

By the eighteenth century, the scientific study of eclipses in Europe was well advanced. The mathematics pioneered by Kepler and Newton had succeeded in explaining planetary and lunar motions. Many of the associated optical phenomena of the eclipse were also understood. Color changes to the Moon during lunar eclipses and the presence of the solar chromosphere and corona were all worthy of further study.

In 1780, Samuel Wilkins, an American, became one of the first to travel a great distance with the express purpose of eclipse observation. Unfortunately, for all his trouble, he seems to have missed the path of solar totality due to a mathematical error.

Later eclipse astronomers traveled to Australia in 1857, Peru in 1858, and the eastern Pacific and Spain in 1860. Some of these expeditions were bedeviled by clouds; others, by observational problems or nasty local insects. The greatest success of the period was enjoyed by a British team in Spain that pioneered methods of eclipse photography.

In 1868, spectrophotography was used by a French expedition in India. They demonstrated that prominences were mostly hydrogen gas. A British team investigating the same eclipse discovered the element helium. The English team did not fare as well in 1870. During their sea voyage to observe an eclipse from Sicily, their vessel was wrecked. Happily, no lives or equipment was lost. The French solar astronomers, after a daring escape from the besieged city of Paris by hot air balloon, were sadly defeated by clouds during their attempt to observe the 1870 solar eclipse.

Later nineteenth-century expeditions experienced a similar pattern of good luck and misfortune. Perhaps the saddest fate was the death of an experienced eclipse observer from dysentery during a British expedition to the West Indies in 1889.

The crowning moment of the era of the eclipse explorer was the 1919 validation of Einstein's theory of general relativity. From the South American coast, solar eclipse photographs were taken to investigate shifts in position of stars close to the solar disk. Largely because these correlated closely with the predictions of relativity theory, Einstein ultimately received a Nobel Prize.

Eclipses and Associated Phenomena

To help understand the basic cause of the eclipse, you might refer to a simple drawing of the Earth–Moon–Sun system. Such an illustration, which is not to scale, is provided in Figure 7–3. Scale would have been an elusive goal in such a representation because of the vast difference in relative distances and sizes among the three bodies involved. The center-to-center Earth–Moon separation is typically 236,000 miles. As discussed in Chapter 4, the Moon's orbit around Earth is actually somewhat elliptical, which (as discussed shortly) has a bearing upon eclipses. The Earth–Sun separation is much larger—about 93 million miles.

In terms of relative size, the Moon has a radius of slightly more than 1,000 miles. Earth's radius is close to 4,000 miles. The radius of the photosphere, the visible solar surface, is more than 100 times Earth's radius!

By a fluke of orbital position and relative physical sizes, both the Sun and the Moon subtend almost exactly the same angle in the sky—about ½ a degree of arc. This means that during an eclipse of the Sun, the Moon can almost exactly cover the photosphere.

By considering the extreme rays of sunlight striking the Moon during a solar eclipse (as shown in Figure 7–3), it is possible to denote the two portions of the shadow cast by the Moon on Earth—the umbra and the penumbra. A person standing in the central part of the shadow, or umbra, on Earth's surface will experience a total solar eclipse. Observers located in the much broader penumbra will experience a partial solar eclipse.

If the Moon is close to the apogee (the farthest distance from Earth) of its elliptical orbit around Earth during the eclipse, its distance from Earth is great enough so that the umbra will not strike Earth's surface. In such an annular eclipse, the Moon does not entirely cover the Sun; part of the Sun is visible during the eclipse as a bright ring surrounding the Moon.

The region of Earth's surface within the umbra is never very wide; typically it is about 75 miles. Because of the umbra's high speed across Earth's surface (1,000 to 2,000 miles per hour), the duration of the total phase of a solar eclipse is never greater than 8 minutes.

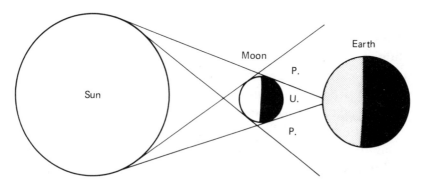

Figure 7–3 Alignment of the Sun, Moon, and Earth for a solar eclipse (*Note:* Umbra and penumbra are abbrevated by "U." and "P." Distances and sizes are not to scale. In a lunar eclipse, the positions of the Moon and Earth are interchanged.)

Solar eclipses are not very frequent at any given location. For example, suppose that you have funded the construction of a massive solar observatory in your town to view an upcoming eclipse of the Sun. If the eclipse is rained out, you need only wait for the next total solar eclipse in your location to recoup your investment. Make sure you have patient backers, however, because the average wait for the next exact repetition of solar eclipse location is around 400 years! Total solar eclipses occur somewhere on Earth at intervals of about 18 months. Partial eclipses are more common; about three occur each year somewhere on our planet.

In an eclipse of the Moon, the objects line up with Earth between the Sun and Moon. Earth, being larger, casts a wider shadow than does the Moon. Earth's shadow is actually about 3 times the size of the Moon at the typical Earth-Moon separation. Therefore, the duration of a lunar eclipse is consequently greater than that of a solar eclipse. Lunar eclipse totality can also be viewed over a greater area of Earth's surface than can solar eclipse totality.

Because of the physical properties of the three celestial objects involved in the eclipse, a number of interesting phenomena are associated with solar and lunar eclipses. First among these is the phase of the Moon. Solar eclipses always occur when the Moon is new; lunar eclipses occur when the Moon is full.

During an eclipse of the Moon, the predominant effect is an alteration in the normal grayish yellow color of the full moon. For a shallow lunar eclipse, the Moon will be an orange or a coppery hue and be very bright. At the border of the umbra and penumbra, a bluish tint will be visible. A somewhat deeper eclipse results in a full moon with a brick red color and a grayish yellow boundary between the two shadow zones. Still deeper eclipses cause the Moon to have a ruddy or dark red color. The umbra may have a dark center. If the lunar eclipse is even more intense, lunar surface features become harder to discern and the Moon's color is brown or dark gray. Finally, the deepest lunar eclipse results in a nearly invisible moon at mid-eclipse. During the more intense lunar eclipses, more stars than usual will be visible in the vicinity of the dimmed Moon.

Some of the factors contributing to the intensity of a lunar eclipse are celestial—for example, Earth–Moon separation and the location of the terrestrial observer relative to the umbra–penumbra boundary. Because Earth, with its changeable atmosphere, is also involved in the lunar eclipse process, atmospheric factors can also influence the intensity of a lunar eclipse. Dust in the atmosphere, for example, can enlarge Earth's shadow and deepen a lunar eclipse. This dust may result from a variety of terrestrial and extraterrestrial causes, such as forest fires, volcanic eruptions, and meteor showers. Although difficult to predict in advance, the intensity of a lunar eclipse can be utilized to monitor our life-sustaining ocean of air.

Solar eclipses, although shorter in duration, are optically more impressive than lunar eclipses. During the brief moments of totality, the Sun's visible surface (the photosphere) is covered by the Moon's disk. The Sun's lower atmosphere (the chromosphere) may be visible around the Moon's disk just as the eclipse begins and ends. During totality, the more extensive and tenuous outer atmosphere of the Sun (the corona) becomes observable. Before the invention of solar telescopes equipped with occulting fingers to dim the photosphere's image, all of our knowledge of the chromosphere and corona was obtained during total solar eclipses.

As the sky darkens during a total eclipse of the Sun, stars appear in the sky. Some of these may be quite close to the solar disk. Also during a total eclipse of the Sun, it may be possible to view prominences, those portions of the chromosphere pulled temporarily out from the Sun's visible disk by interaction with the Sun's magnetic field. Another fascinating phenomenon, first noted by British astronomer Francis Baily in 1836, is Baily's beads. Manifested as a bright necklace of lights around portions of the lunar disk, this phenomenon is caused by sunlight passing through valleys in the lunar highlands.

Eclipse Observation

For naked-eye viewing of partial solar eclipses, smoked glass or similar optical filters are required. Unless the Sun is very close to the horizon, you should never attempt to view even the partially eclipsed Sun with the unprotected naked eye or through an unfiltered telescope.

For the more frequent and longer-duration lunar eclipse, tripod-mounted binoculars and small telescopes are the best observing tools. To photograph a lunar eclipse, some experienced hands recommend a telephoto lens in place of a telescope–camera combination. For fairly short-duration exposures, a clock drive may not be necessary. Lunar eclipse photography is not easy and requires some practice. However, it is very significant in light of the fact that the color of the Moon during totality yields information regarding the state of Earth's atmosphere.

ECLIPSE ACTIVITY

Lunar Eclipse Photography

To attempt lunar eclipse close-up photography, you could use a tripod-mounted telephoto lens with a focal length longer than 200 mm. During the partial phases of the eclipse, typical daytime exposures are sufficient since the full moon is still partially illuminated by sunlight. As the eclipse deepens toward totality, exposures of a minute or more are required. Because of the long duration of lunar eclipses, you could experiment with a wide variety of exposures in both color and black and white.

If you become proficient at lunar eclipse photography, you can turn this into a valuable astronomical activity. An irregular-appearing eclipsed Moon is evidence of large storms and cloud patterns in Earth's atmosphere. A large amount of volcanic dust in Earth's atmosphere will produce a reddish eclipsed Moon. Particularly beautiful eclipse photos by amateurs are often published in the "Gallery" section of *Sky & Telescope* along with the settings and exposure times used.   ■

CHAPTER 8

Visitors in the Sky

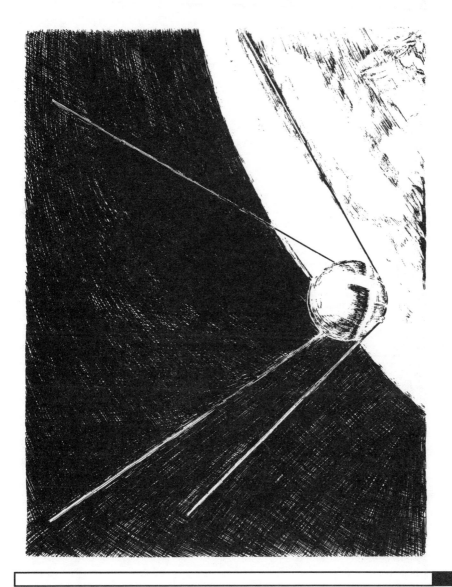

Year of comets and meteors transient and
    strange—lo! even here one equally transient and
    strange!
As I flit through you hastily, soon to fall and be
    gone, what is this chant,
What am I myself but one of your meteors?
    —Walt Whitman, *Year of Meteors* (1859–1860)

There is a class of celestial objects that occasionally visit our skies and are observable from urban observing locations. These transient sky events include meteors, comets, and artificial earth-satellites. Patience and planning are required to observe these celestial visitors, but the results can be gratifying and delightful.

Hot Rocks and Falling Ice

Long before humans entered space, denizens of interplanetary space reached Earth. For centuries, people marveled at the phenomenon of the "shooting star." We now know that shooting stars are produced when ice particles from a passing comet's tail enter Earth's atmosphere and burn up. To early observers, shooting stars were dramatic and scary events. Observers wondered for centuries whether they properly belonged to the atmosphere or to the dark spaces beyond.

As fascinating as the nature of the shooting star, or meteor, is the interaction between the meteorite and human civilization. (A meteorite is an object from space that survives passage through

Earth's atmosphere.) If iron-rich meteoritic bodies from deep space had not survived their fiery tumble to Earth, Iron Age civilization might have been indefinitely delayed.

When a large object from space reached Earth's surface, a readily minable deposit of iron instantly became available. In certain regions, such iron meteorites actually became religious objects. Much of the religious power of Delphi, the home of the ancient Greek oracles, is thought to have been due to a sacred stone called the *Omphalos*. According to astroarchaeologist Gerald Hawkins, this sacred object was a meteorite.

Thousands of years earlier, a much more massive rock from space carved the famous Meteor Crater in Arizona. Some American Indian legends consider it wise to shun the site of the impact. Every 1,000 years or so, a meteorite of equivalent size falls and impacts with more destructive force than the world's nuclear arsenals combined. Fortunately for evolving civilization, most past impacts occurred in the wilderness or ocean. But unless we apply modern technology to give warning of these approaching large, rocky invaders from the skies, the "global village" of future centuries will certainly pay the price.

Various peoples have considered these rocks from space to be imbued with divine powers. In the pre-Columbian western hemisphere, at least one meteorite was buried ceremoniously after being wrapped in mummy cloth! Some astronomers suspect that the holy Kaaba in Mecca, one of the centerpiece shrines of Islam, contains a stone meteorite.

Today, in many museum collections, we can visit the remnants of ancient and modern fiery impacts. Although still very impressive, these meteorites have been greatly reduced by the heat of their entry into Earth's atmosphere. Many of them have also been fragmented by the force of impact.

Modern scientists are quite confident that they understand the phenomena of meteorites and shooting stars. Although definitely quite awe-inspiring, these celestial objects properly belong to the interplay of the physical, natural universe rather than to the intervention of the divine.

Shooting stars are ephemeral events occurring when a chip of cosmic dust (with a mass measured in grams) encounters Earth's atmosphere and burns up at an altitude of 50 or 60 miles. Although some of these can be seen to fall every night, most meteors occur in well-defined and predictable showers. These meteor showers are the intersections of Earth's orbit around the Sun with clouds of dust and ice emitted from comet tails.

No meteor has ever reached the ground, although some samples of cosmic dust have been collected by high-flying rockets and aircraft. The magnificent collections of meteorites (some weighing in at a ton or more) in museum repositories such as that at the New York Museum of Natural History have an entirely different origin.

Early in the history of the Solar System, about 4,600 million years ago, the Sun and planets condensed from a primeval gas cloud or nebula. Fragments of this gaseous material condensed a great distance from the Sun. Instead of forming into major planets, thousands of extremely small rocky chunks called *asteroids* formed and circled the Sun between the orbits of Mars and Jupiter. Although this "asteroid belt" is the home of most asteroids, some of them approach the Sun more closely.

In early science fiction epics, the asteroid belt was a place of peril for terrestrial space travelers. Human ships were often holed like the *Titanic* in futile attempts to run the gauntlet of the celestial "rockbergs." Space pirates, waiting to trap the unwary wayfarer, would lurk behind convenient rocks. In some popular movies, strange life forms have evolved amid the asteroids, which adds to the peril and fascination of this zone.

As space probes *Pioneer X* and *XI* and *Voyager 1* and *2* traversed the asteroid belt on their way into the interstellar night, they found a much more prosaic reality. There were no rockbergs. Although thousands of asteroids are known to exist with diameters ranging from miles to hundreds of miles, they are scattered through billions of cubic miles of interplanetary space. The frequency of dust impacts, let alone rock impacts, experienced by these early extraplanetary robots was not appreciably higher in the belt than elsewhere in the Solar System.

However, the asteroids have been around for almost 5,000 billion years. Subject to the gravitational perturbations caused by the proximity of nearby, massive Jupiter, some of them have had their orbits altered many times. High-speed collisions between asteroids must have occasionally occurred, spewing rocky debris throughout the Solar System. Some of these rocks are large enough to survive the passage through Earth's atmosphere (and be classified as meteorites) if they chance upon our terrestrial orb. Meteor Crater and the crater-scarred face of our Moon give witness to the large size of some of these wandering projectiles.

ACTIVITY 1

Asteroid Viewing

Unfortunately, it is difficult, at least from an urban viewing station, to observe the largest asteroids. The brightest of them, Vesta, is the only asteroid visible to the naked eye. At its brightest, Vesta has an apparent visual magnitude of 5.1. Four other asteroids have visual magnitudes between 6 and 7 and are therefore, easily visible in binoculars or a small telescope. These are Pallas, Ceres, Iris, and Eros. Ceres, the largest known asteroid, has a diameter of about 600 miles. From an urban site, these asteroids can be observed under good seeing conditions if you know exactly where to look. Asteroid visibility information is often published in *Sky & Telescope*. Because of their great distance and small size, all asteroids will seem starlike through your binoculars or small telescope. ∎

Sometimes, asteroids and fragments from asteroidal collisions approach Earth closely. Purely by accident, an amateur astronomer obtained impressive photographic evidence of an asteroidal "near-miss" in 1972. An impressive bolide, or fireball, was observed to leave a trail in the atmosphere from Utah to Alberta, Canada. We were fortunate at that time since the intruder "skipped" out of the atmosphere. If its "aim" had been very slightly different (in cosmic terms), the 1972 bolide would have impacted Salt Lake City with the destructive force of a small atomic bomb!

No sky observer can plan for the observation of such a rare event. However, you can plan observing sessions to correspond with "scheduled" appearances of meteor showers.

ACTIVITY 2

The Meteor Party

Shooting stars, or meteors, are apparently remnants from a comet's passage through interplanetary space. As such, they seem to radiate from the same point, or radiant, in the sky. In planning a serious meteor party, it might be a good idea to sketch a map of the evening sky with the constellation containing the radiant clearly labeled.

You might wish to base your sky sketch upon pictured locations of bright stars from a star catalog or skychart. Each person participating in your meteor party should have a copy of the sky sketch. A list of the major Northern Hemisphere meteor showers is provided in Appendix 2. Unless you are impervious to the elements or live in a near-tropical clime, your favorite meteor showers will probably be the Lyrids, Eta Aquarids, Delta Aquarids, Perseids, and Orionids, which occur in the warmer months.

The Earth-impact speed of the dust and ice particles that become meteors depends upon the dynamics of the orbits of Earth and the particle stream. Speeds vary between 33,000 and 145,000 miles per hour.

Those short-period comets known to be associated with these events are also listed in Appendix 2. Note that the number of meteors expected per hour is for a sky in which magnitude 6 stars are visible. You will probably not see as many from an urban viewing location.

If you are including star, planet, and Moon gazing in your meteor event, bring your telescope and binoculars. However, the best instruments for observing meteors are those permanently mounted below your forehead.

If you are interested in coordinating your meteor shower observations with those of other observers, you should synchronize your watch with standard time signals provided by commercial radio, shortwave radio, or the local telephone company. This will allow data from widely separated observers to be applied to the same meteor when it is observed from different vantage points. Also, if friends are assisting you, it pays for each to concentrate upon a different portion of the sky.

All meteor observers should be equipped with a comfortable lounge chair and with sky sketches attached to clipboards. Flashlights used to illuminate the sky sketches while meteor tracks and their corresponding times are recorded should be covered in red-tinted plastic so that the night sensitivity of the observers' eyes is not degraded.

During the few hours that you lie in the lounge chairs and wait for the occasional meteor, it is nice to have friends around to chat with. Also, liquids and snacks are a good idea. It would be a critical mistake, at least during the summer, to forget the bug repellent! Even during the summer meteor showers, it pays to bring along a sweater in case the temperature drops.

If you become a serious meteor observer, try to record the visual apparent magnitude of each meteor as well as its track. You can do this by comparing each meteor to the nearest stars. Another piece of information necessary for the scientific study of your shooting star is the record of the exact time of the event.

To do really serious work, coordinate your observations with friends at a number of widely separated sites. Ideally, these observation stations should be separated by 10 to 20 miles. Because meteors burn out about 60 miles overhead, such a baseline may allow triangulation of meteor observations. By comparing observations of the same meteor from two or more sites to the positions of nearby stars, anyone conversant in high school trigonometry can estimate the height of the shooting star. Meteor triangulation is discussed further in Appendix 3.

If you are planning a meteor shower activity, it pays to review the necessary steps:

1. Prepare skycharts of the region of the heavens from which the meteors are predicted to radiate.

2. Check in advance to make sure that streetlights or buildings do not obscure the portion of the sky that will contain most meteor tracks.

3. Obtain a comfortable lounge chair for every observer.

4. Make sure to take along extra clothing, bug repellent, drinks, and snacks.

5. Make sure that one or more sharpened pencils are attached to each clipboard along with the skycharts.

6. Be very sure that all flashlights have red filters.

Because of the large number of meteors and the relative paucity of funded astronomers, serious meteor observation is almost an exclusive domain of the amateur. An urban meteor observer will of course not see the number reported by rural meteor observers, but even observations of only the brightest meteors in a shower are of value. A number of clearinghouses of meteor records exist. One is the American Meteor Society, Department of Physics and Astronomy, State University of New York (SUNY), Genesco, New York 14454.

If you are very fortunate, you may someday view a really impressive fireball. Such an event in the United States should be reported to the Smithsonian Institution in Washington, D.C. In Canada, you should contact the Herzberg Institute of Astrophysics in Ottawa. If the fireball is audible, try to report quickly. An impact may have occurred nearby and fresh meteorites are of much greater scientific value than older ones! ∎

As impressive as they are, the ephemeral shooting star and even the city-destroying meteorite pale into insignificance when they are compared to another temporary sky event. This is the passage of a comet during one of its brief, recurrent visits to the inner Solar System.

Comets: Swords in the Sky

To prescientific people, nothing was more frightening than the appearance of a "hairy star" that sometimes seemed to look like a sword hanging in the sky. The unpredicted appearance (or apparition) of a comet has occasionally influenced human history. The panic among the English Saxons when Halley's comet appeared over northern Europe in the eleventh century may have contributed to the victory of the Normans in 1066 at the Battle of Hastings. Halley's comet, which belongs to the class of periodic comets, returns to our skies every 76 years.

Modern astronomers are not as frightened of comets as were their more superstitious predecessors, but they are just as fascinated. They know that for most of its existence, a comet is a celestial iceberg orbiting many billions of miles from the Sun. During this part of the comet's existence, layers of ice circle a rocky nucleus that has a diameter measured in tens of miles. When a comet in a highly elliptical orbit enters the inner reaches of the Solar System during the perihelion approach (closest point to the Sun), the heat of absorbed sunlight causes some of the ice to melt and form a roughly spherical halo, or coma, which can be tens of thousands of miles in diameter.

Solar radiation pressure then pushes evaporated particles of methane, ammonia, and water-ice out from the Sun to form the comet's tail. This tail, which can be 100 million miles in length, always points away from the Sun. Although very dramatic, the comet's tail is also quite tenuous. All of the material in a typical comet tail could be packed into a few large suitcases!

Even stranger is humanity's relationship with the visitor that may have balefully illuminated the fields of Hastings. Long associated with war and suffering, Halley's comet would become the target of a flotilla of peaceful spacecraft as most of the spacefaring powers of twentieth-century Earth cooperated in the preliminary exploration of this mysterious visitor.

The Comet in Myth and History

The word *comet* itself is derived from the Greek word for *hair*. Like the Chinese, the Tshi people of Zaire consider comets to be "hairy stars." The Aztecs of pre-Columbian Mezoamerica, perhaps influenced by tobacco, saw comets as "smoking stars." Closer to the truth is the conception of the Tongans, who view comets as "dusty stars."

Although comets were considered by many precivilized and early civilized peoples to be messengers of the celestial gods, few or none of their mythologies treat these gossamery wisps to be good omens. To the Masai, the comet is a portent of famine; to their African neighbors, the Eghap and the Djaga, a visible comet warns of epidemic disease. To the Luba, also of Africa, the comet signifies the death of a leader.

Today, few people believe the ancient stories about the baleful influence of comets. (Even during the 1910 apparition of Halley's comet, however, some people feared the effects of gaseous emanations from the comet's tail.) Although we realize that the day-to-day affairs of terrestrials are not influenced by the motions of comets (or other celestial bodies), we have also learned that these objects have greatly influenced the evolution of our planet and its atmosphere. Without comets, in fact, neither humans nor other terrestrial life forms might exist.

Comets and Evolution

In the beginning, as the Sun and planets condensed from the great solar nebula, the Solar System contained more ice, dust, and rock than it does at present. At least in the early planetary environment, space was far from empty. The inner reaches of the Solar System must have been crossed by the eccentric tracks of a great many icy bodies as they orbited the central accumulation that would someday become the Sun. These objects, or protocomets, may have condensed out of the contracting solar nebula before the planets and their satellites.

We can have no direct knowledge of the sizes of these protocomets. Perhaps they consisted of rocky nuclei a few miles across covered with layers of methane, ammonia, and water-ice, as do present-day comets when they are far from the Sun. Or perhaps they were more like some of the satellites of outer planets, which are much larger objects also consisting of rock and ice.

After the Sun reached its thermonuclear ignition point, the light from the infant star would have heated the hydrogen/helium atmospheres of the inner planets. Over millions of years, these gases were evaporated into space. While this was happening, the streams of light and electrically charged particles emanating from the Sun began the process of clearing dust and gas from the inner Solar System.

The inner planets (Mercury, Venus, Earth, and Mars) were cooling as they condensed. As the primeval planetary atmospheres escaped to space, protocomets must have regularly smacked into these new worlds. On Earth and Venus, extensive atmospheres have largely eroded the scars of these impacts in the 4,600 million years or so since they occurred. Mercury, Mars, and the Moon still bear the scars of these titanic collisions.

157

Earth was still lifeless in this era. Time after time, giant comets must have flamed across the skies, only to impact on the cooling crust of our newborn world. Rain must have fallen after each impact, only to be evaporated quickly by the high temperatures of the still nearly molten planet.

Gradually, the planet cooled and oceans could form. The frequency of cometary impacts diminished as the inner Solar System became cleared of these projectiles. The energy of sunlight began to power the chemical factory of Earth's atmosphere. Atmospheric carbon dioxide evolved from cometary methane; nitrogen in our planet's atmosphere was produced from ammonia; and the oceans formed from cometary water. Finally, conditions were just right for a miracle to occur in the shallow seas of Earth—an event that we may never entirely understand. Somehow, from a primeval soup of chemicals in warm water, bathed in a sea of solar radiation, the first living cell developed.

Even after photosynthesis had converted most of the atmospheric carbon dioxide resulting from the cometary bombardment into oxygen, comets may have played a considerable role in the evolution of Earth's biosphere. Periodically, life on Earth seems to undergo mass extinctions. Since sedimentary rock layers coincident with the mass extinctions in the fossil record often seem to contain cosmic rather than terrestrial quantities of iridium, many scientists have reasoned that a contributory factor to the mass extinctions may have been "comet storms."

Whether such comet storms are due to a possible companion star to our Sun nicknamed "Nemesis" as some scientists have speculated, to the chance interactions between the Solar System and nearby interstellar dust clouds as others have suggested, or to some other factor is unknown at present. But if the cometary extinction theory is correct, humans and all higher mammals may owe their lives to a comet storm that may have obliterated the last of the dinosaurs at the end of the Cretaceous period about 65 million years ago.

Almost all scientists accept the link between comets and the early evolution of Earth's atmosphere, and a majority would probably consider the evidence for a cometary contribution to the Cretaceous extinction to be more than circumstantial. Only a few, however, cling to the belief that the cometary influence goes deeper.

One of these is Cornell astronomer Thomas Gold. Professor Gold is a proponent of the unconventional theory that much of Earth's fossil fuel reserve is due to cometary impacts and is not the remains of long-dead marine organisms. Very recently, Professor Gold's theory was tested in Sweden, where a gas well was drilled more than 4 miles down in a 368-million-year-old, 30-mile-wide impact crater. Although the first $40-million hole came up dry, Gold's iconoclastic theory will certainly be tested again. Even though it may be a long shot, it predicts hydrocarbon reserves that would be of enormous use to the world economy if they exist.

The Oort Comet Cloud

Astronomers have long wondered about the source of comets in the modern Solar System. They know of two basic classes of comets—recurrent or periodic comets that return to the inner Solar System at intervals of years or decades and long-period comets that travel in extremely elliptical orbits and require tens of thousands of years to make one circuit of the Sun.

In 1950, the Dutch astronomer Jan Hendrik Oort published an analysis of the known long-period comets. He demonstrated that most of their orbits seem to originate a distance greater than or equal to 20,000 astronomical units from the Sun. (One astronomical unit, or AU, is the mean Earth–Sun distance, or about 93 million miles.) More recent work indicates that the typical aphelion (most distant point from the Sun) of a long-period comet is actually closer to 50,000 AU, almost 20 percent of the distance to our Solar System's nearest stellar neighbor!

Comets must have formed in the outer reaches of the condensing solar nebula about 5,000 million years ago. As such, comet nuclei contain perhaps the most ancient unaltered solid material in our Solar System.

At intervals of a million years or so, as our Sun revolves around the center of the Milky Way Galaxy, another star travels within the outer limits of the Oort comet cloud. Some comets are ejected from the Solar System during these close stellar encounters, others are pushed sunward.

Some of these cometary visitors to the inner Solar System head directly out once again into the outer depths, the paths of others are influenced by the gravitational fields of the giant planets Jupiter and Saturn. Both of these worlds have "families" of short-period comets.

There is some evidence that comet orbits change further as these objects make repeated passes through the inner Solar System. Some of them may ultimately lose much of their layered ice and dust and settle into nearly circular orbits similar to those of asteroids.

Unlike the planets and asteroids, however, comets are not confined to the narrow layer of the ecliptic. They may enter the inner Solar System from any location on the celestial sphere, which indicates that they condensed before the solar nebula became disk shaped.

Observable Aspects of Comets

Comets, when cooperative, put on a dramatic sky show. The coma of evaporated ice is tens of thousands of miles in diameter and looks like a celestial nebula that may change from night to night. Snaking back from the halolike coma is the immense tail of the comet, which can be 100 million miles in length. Two causes produce the striking tail. First, solar radiation is absorbed in the volatile layers of ice that circle the comet's rocky nucleus. Then, solar radiation pressure pushes some of this material out of the coma into the tail. Cometary tails are so thin that they are partially transparent to starlight shining from behind.

Particularly dramatic cometary apparitions, such as Halley's comet in 1910, are clearly visible to the unaided eye. For others, you need a pair of binoculars or a telescope to resolve the coma as a "fuzzy star" and to observe the tail. The appearance of both of these cometary aspects may change rapidly as the comet nears perihelion.

Some comets have more than one tail. Multiple tails may indicate the presence of extensive dust layers as well as ice around the nucleus.

Around the rocky nucleus, which is only a few miles in diameter, is a spherical coma of gas that is tens of thousands of miles in diameter. Although it is invisible to terrestrial eyes, spacecraft have returned excellent data about the extensive hydrogen cloud that surrounds the coma when the comet is close to perihelion.

Earthbound astronomers often lose sight of a comet in the glare of the Sun just before perihelion. If the perihelion distance is very close (0.1 AU or less), the comet may emerge in greatly altered form. Some "sungrazers" have been known to split into several independent comets after a very close perihelion pass. At least one sungrazer has been observed by a spacecraft to actually impact the Sun!

At least once every decade, an enormous comet from the Oort cloud passes through the inner Solar System. Although high hopes existed for dramatic sky shows, Comet Kohoutek in 1973–1974 and Comet Austin in 1990 were visual duds perhaps because these long-period comets were making their first visit to the inner Solar System and still had an extensive dust sheath. If we can wait patiently for their next perihelion passages in A.D. 50,000 or so, the sky show will be much more dramatic!

To observers in the Northern Hemisphere, the 1986 apparition of Halley's comet was decidedly less than spectacular. Cosmonauts aboard *Mir*, robot spacecraft of the "international Halley flotilla," and sky observers in the Southern Hemisphere did much better. However, some of the scheduled Halley watches in New York's Prospect Park and elsewhere did produce some telescopic views of the comet in amateur instruments of modest aperture.

In the far future, we may live on these celestial objects or mine them. Someday, some comets may even be covered with genetically modified trees, and we may hitchhike on these little forested worlds on 50,000-year odysseys to the stars. Conceived by physicist Freeman Dyson, this concept of habitable comets offers the possibility that the universe is quite friendly to life. Because comets are separated by billions of miles (as opposed to the trillions of miles between neighboring stars), travel between life-supporting cometary oases in the interstellar wilderness may

161

require treks of decades rather than the centuries or millennia required to travel to the nearest star. Someday, more people may actually be living in the Oort cloud than on Earth and other planets. Perhaps they will occasionally visit us on holiday and preserve Earth as a "nature park."

In the meantime, urban astronomers can be certain that once every decade or so, a visible comet will grace (or curse?) the night sky. As well as conducting very well-attended comet watches, amateur astronomers can provide a real service to the professionals by keeping track of day-to-day changes in a visible comet's tail(s), color, brightness, and shape.

ACTIVITY 3

Observing Comets

If your local newspapers or astronomy magazines predict a visible apparition for a comet, you can attempt observations from a suitably dark urban setting. Usually, finder charts are published in *Sky & Telescope* and *Astronomy* magazines so that you can track the intruder to the inner Solar System against the stellar background.

One way to use the published finder charts is to estimate the comet's predicted position relative to nearby bright stars. Because a wide field of view is better in comet observing, high-magnification binoculars or a wide-field Newtonian might be your instrument of choice.

You might try sketching the comet on a day-to-day basis. This will give you a record of the coma's changing shape and some indication of when the tail "turns on." To monitor a comet's brightness, you could compare it to nearby stars of known visual apparent magnitude. You could compare its color with that of nearby stars, or you could check its visibility through filters of various colors. ∎

One reason why your observations of comets will be of great value is the difficulty in predicting a comet's visual performance in advance. A host of variables—for example, comet perihelion distance, the number of previous passes through the inner Solar System, and relative Earth/comet/Sun positions near cometary perihelion—conspire to make comet brightness predictions inaccurate. A great deal of observational data, coupled with new theories, will ultimately improve our understanding of these "swords in the sky."

Inhabited Stars

Sooner or later, many amateur astronomers become interested in observing humanity's impact on the heavens. Since the beginning of the space age, thousands of objects have been placed (at least temporarily) beyond the reach of Earth's atmosphere. Many of these have been observable through binoculars, small telescopes, or the unaided human eye.

As has been demonstrated by countless pictures beamed down by astronauts and cosmonauts, one characteristic of the orbital environment is "weightlessness." This characteristic is not caused by the fact that the spacecraft and its occupants are hundreds or thousands of miles above Earth's surface. Instead, weightlessness is due to the fact that Earth's gravitational attraction, which tends to pull the spacecraft back to Earth, is exactly balanced by the craft's "inertia," which tends to direct it out into space on a constant-speed straight-line trajectory. The closed path resulting from this balance is the satellite's orbit.

Unless a satellite orbits so close to Earth's surface (about 100 miles above it) that its orbit is affected by atmospheric drag or if it is a low-mass orbital balloon that can be "perturbed" by solar radiation pressure, Kepler's laws (see Chapter 5) are a very good approximation to the motion of a satellite around Earth.

The high and low points of a satellite's orbit are respectively called the *apogee* and *perigee*. At perigee, the satellite's orbital velocity will be higher than at apogee.

It takes a good deal of energy to place something in a closed loop around Earth at more than 100 miles above the surface. The spacecraft must lift off from Earth's surface and accelerate to an orbital velocity of 18,000 miles per hour (around 5 miles per second). Although other approaches have been suggested, the only practical method of accomplishing this task today is the chemical rocket.

One very popular orbital path is near or along the equator. Rocket designers can save some energy (and therefore money) by launching eastward along this track and getting an extra boost from Earth's orbital motion. Satellites in equatorial orbits are generally observed in the east or west portion of the evening sky.

American reconnaissance satellites and most Soviet craft fly along a path that takes them over or near Earth's poles. Polar-orbiting craft travel along a north–south track.

Low-orbit satellites require approximately 90 minutes to complete one orbit around Earth's center of mass. Communications satellites are typically placed 22,400 miles above Earth's surface in an equatorial orbit. The orbital period at such a location is 24 hours. With a small amount of course correction to compensate for perturbations, a communications satellite in such a geosynchronous orbit will seen to be suspended indefinitely above the same spot on Earth's surface. As geosynchronous communications platforms become larger, it will become possible to view them with low magnification as starlike points that seem to be stationary.

To totally escape from Earth's gravity and enter orbit around the Sun, the low-orbiting satellite must have its speed increased from 5 miles per second to 7 miles per second (around 25,000 miles per hour). The "human speed record" is currently held by those Apollo astronauts who achieved near-escape velocity en route to the Moon.

ACTIVITY 4

Observing Artificial Satellites

To observe an artificial earth-satellite from an urban location, you need a location that is moderately light-free and is not too obstructed near the horizon over which the satellite rises or sets. Generally, telescope clock drives will be extraneous unless you have very expensive equipment that allows you to greatly vary drive rate. Remember, a satellite does not move with the diurnal motion of the stars or planets.

The naked eye is perhaps the best tool to use in observing a satellite. Binoculars or a telescope eyepiece of very low magnification (high field or view) is generally quite sufficient. These instruments are usually not enough to view really small objects, such as the first earth-satellites, from an urban location. But, this is no problem! Today, there are quite a few artificial large objects in space from which to choose. A moderately large orbiting satellite will often be seen as magnitude 3 or brighter.

Low-orbiting satellites are usually visible low in the sky and move at a speed such that they will seem to cross the sky in a few minutes. Low in the observer's sky shortly after dusk or before dawn, a low-orbiting satellite is in position to catch sunlight and reflect it to the observer while it is in a sky background still dark enough so that it is visible.

If the satellite suddenly "blinks off" from view and becomes invisible, then the relative positions of satellite/observer/Sun have changed so that reflected sunlight from the craft no longer reaches the observer. Some satellites seem to rapidly scintillate or "twinkle" as you observe them. This effect is due to sunlight reflecting off irregular structures on the spacecraft as the spacecraft spins.

In observing a satellite, you might try to gauge these pulsations. By comparing the moving image to nearby stars, what are the maximum and minimum visual apparent magnitudes of the spacecraft? How many times per minute does the brightness vary and are the variations constant?

Unless you have access to published orbital predictions for the satellite under consideration and your location, most satellite observations will be serendipitous. But if you become systematic with your satellite observation strategy, you will be prepared to render a great service to scientists studying Earth's upper atmosphere. ■

ACTIVITY 5

Observing Artificial Comets

Sometimes, robot and peopled spacecraft deposit barium clouds or other gaseous material in Earth's upper atmosphere. Reflecting sunlight to observers over distances measured in hundreds or thousands of miles, these clouds can appear brighter than magnitude 2 and elicit many UFO reports. If you read about a forthcoming "artificial comet" of this type in your local newspaper, you might try to observe (with binoculars) the duration, shape, and brightness of the cloud. Communicated to the appropriate agency and combined with thousands of other reports, your observational record will be of great use to atmospheric scientists.   ■

Today, we are well into the era of routine human occupation of near-earth orbit. People in cities along the southeastern coast of the United States can often view daytime launches of the space shuttle. Some nighttime launches are visible as far north as the coast of New Jersey! Out west, shuttles returning to the landing strip in the California desert can be tracked by binoculars as they descend through the stratosphere and troposphere. On some entries, the sonic booms of the returning shuttles rattle windows in the cities of southern California.

At the present time, humanity's first permanent space station is nearing completion a few years behind schedule (and probably billions of rubles over budget). Although *Mir* follows an unvarying orbital track, its altitude above Earth's surface sometimes varies. It may drop down a bit to rendezvous with a *Soyuz* ferry or a *Progress* freighter, and its orbit may be moved upward when high solar activity results in greater atmospheric drag.

In its original configuration, *Mir* was about 40 feet in length and was equipped with an array of solar cells spanning about 100 feet. Since its launch in 1986, new modules and solar panels have been added, increasing both its size and visibility. When the Soviet shuttle *Buran* commences regular missions to *Mir*, this craft should be quite visible.

Mir, because of the high inclination of its orbit, is often visible to the naked eye from an urban location. For example, members of the New York chapter of the Space Frontier Society have had success in seeing *Mir* from the deck of the aircraft carrier *Intrepid*, which is docked as a permanent museum at a Hudson River pier in Manhattan.

Because the orbital speed of *Mir* varies as its orbital height is slightly modified, the times of visible passes for this operational space facility cannot be accurately predicted more than a few days in advance. The National Space Society in Washington, D.C., operates a telephone hotline that gives up-to-date predictions of the visible passes that *Mir* makes over North America.

Before the end of the Cold War and the start of the current era of glasnost, the Soviet space program was shrouded in secrecy. Much of our "early warning" regarding Soviet space activity was due to the Kettering Group, radio amateurs who are based at a rural British high school.

Mir often beams signals down to Soviet land- and sea-based receiving centers. One of the Soviet sea-based centers, or comships, has often been located off the northeastern United States; several others are often operating at other North Atlantic locations. Typical *Mir* communication frequencies include 143.625, 166.123, 166.140, and 166.150 MHz. The *Soyuz* ferries typically broadcast on 166.150 MHz. Many radio amateurs in England and North America routinely eavesdrop on these transmissions.

In its final form, the planned American Space Station *Freedom* may be considerably larger than *Mir*. Since *Mir* is easily visible to the naked eye, *Freedom* may, under good observing conditions, outshine all except the brightest stars. As the world space programs gear up for the major expeditions of the next century, small telescopes or binoculars should be sufficient to check up on the progress of construction of lunar and interplanetary craft at these space stations. When the first research and mining towns are established on our airless Moon, the lights of these small cities, shining slightly brighter than earthshine on the dark face of our planet's natural satellite, may be resolvable in small telescopes.

Chapter References and Notes

Introduction: A Historical Perspective

Good treatments of the early history of astronomy, its interaction with human culture, and Stone Age observatories are included in:

Gerald S. Hawkins, *Mindsteps to the Cosmos* (New York: Harper & Row, 1983).

Gerald S. Hawkins, *Stonehenge Decoded* (Garden City, NY: Doubleday, 1965).

Fred Hoyle, *On Stonehenge* (San Francisco: W. H. Freeman, 1977).

Chapter 1. Are Those Lights in the Skies Stars?

For a readable, although slightly technical, discussion of the effects of interstellar and atmospheric absorption on starlight, consult:

Jean Dufay, *Introduction to Astrophysics: The Stars*, trans. from French by Owen Gingerich (New York: Dover, 1964).

Good sources of information regarding Earth's atmosphere, its interaction with light, the greenhouse effect, urban heat island, and other related topics are:

Frederick K. Lutgens and Edward J. Tarbuck, *The Atmosphere* 3rd ed. (Englewood Cliffs, NJ: Prentice-Hall, 1979).

R. A. R. Tricker, *The Science of Clouds* (New York: American Elsevier, 1970).

For more information on refraction and the refractive index of air, consult:

Francis A. Jenkins and Harvey E. White, *Fundamentals of Optics* (New York: McGraw-Hill, 1957).

A good place to read about light pollution and its effects on amateur and professional astronomy is *Sky & Telescope* magazine. In particular, see George Lovi's column in the February 1988 issue and columns by Stephen J. O'Meara and David Crawford in the May 1988 issue. Also see the article by David Crawford and Tim Hunter in the July 1990 issue.

Chapter 2. Patterns in the Sky

George O. Abell, *Exploration of the Universe,* 3rd ed. (New York: Holt, Rinehart, & Winston, 1975).

George Lovi, "The Mists of Antiquity," in "Rambling through the Skies" column, *Sky & Telescope* 79 (April 1990): 407–408.

John Sanford, *Observing the Constellations* (New York: Simon & Schuster, 1989).

Chapter 3. Astronomer's Eyes

A very well-written history of the telescope is Isaac Asimov, *Eyes on the Universe* (Boston: Houghton Mifflin, 1975).

Historical material on telescopic astronomy can also be found in the classic: Lucien Rudaux and G. de Vaucouleurs, *Larousse Encyclopedia of Astronomy* (New York: Prometheus Press, 1959).

For the reader interested in engineering details on telescopes, binoculars, the eye, and other optical systems, a good text is: Warren J. Smith, *Modern Optical Engineering* (New York: McGraw-Hill, 1966).

Basic information on clock drives, setting circles, and telescope operation may be obtained from reading an earlier edition of Ian Ridpath, ed., *Norton's 2000.0 Star Atlas and Reference Handbook* (Belmont MA: Sky Publishing, 1990).

For information on Project STAR and other astronomy-education programs, consult:

Alan M. MacRobert, "Astronomy with a $5 Telescope," in "Backyard Astronomy" column, *Sky & Telescope* 79 (April 1990): 384–387.

Edna DeVore, "National Science Foundation Projects for K–12 Astronomy and Planetarium Education," in "Focus on Education" column, conducted by Mark Sonntag, *The Planetarian* 19, no. 1 (March 1990): 40–41.

Chapter 4. Goddess of the Night

Moon myths and legends are discussed in:

Robert Graves, *The White Goddess* (New York: Farrar, Straus & Giroux, 1948).

Encyclopedia Britannica, 15th ed. (Chicago: Encyclopedia Britannica, 1981).

For a good discussion of "blue moons," see David Allen and Carol Allen, *Eclipse* (Boston: Allen & Unwin, 1987).

An excellent beginner's guide to lunar observation can be found in Herbert S. Zim and Robert H. Baker, *A Golden Guide to the Stars* (New York: Golden Press, 1975).

Although a bit out of date, another good lunar source is Hubert J. Bernhard, Dorothy A. Bennett, and Hugh S. Rice, *New Handbook of the Heavens* (New York: Mentor, 1959).

Excellent modern treatments of the Moon can be found in:

David Baker, *The Henry Holt Guide to Astronomy* (New York: Henry Holt, 1978).

Donald H. Menzel and Jay M. Pasachoff, *A Field Guide to Stars and Planets*, 2nd ed. (Boston: Houghton Mifflin, 1983).

The first reference has been magnificently illustrated by British space artist David Hardy; the second by Wil Tirion.

Results of early space age lunar cartography are summarized in H. P. Wilkins, *Moon Maps* (New York: Macmillan, 1960).

Experiences and opinions of a seasoned lunar observer are summarized in two books:

Val A. Firsoff, *The Old Moon and the New* (New York: A. S. Barnes, 1970).

Val A. Firsoff, *Strange World of the Moon* (New York: Basic Books, 1959).

The long and vociferous debate between proponents of the impact and volcano points of view are discussed.

For more information on observation of grazing lunar occultations, consult Grant Fjermedal, *New Horizons in Amateur Astronomy* (New York: Putnam, 1989).

Chapter 5. Wandering Stars: The Planets of Our Solar System

John C. Brandt and Stephen P. Maran, *New Horizons in Astronomy* (San Francisco: W. H. Freeman, 1972).

Gunter D. Roth, *Handbook for Planet Observers*, trans. from the German by Alex Helm (New York: Van Nostrand Reinhold, 1970).

For a good introduction to planetary motions, see R. A. R. Tricker, *Paths of the Planets* (New York: American Elsevier, 1967).

Many tips on planet observation are included in P. Clay Sherrod and Thomas L. Koed, *A Complete Manual of Amateur Astronomy* (New York: Prentice-Hall, 1981).

Chapter 6. Unusual Stars

A very readable reference dealing in part with stellar evolution is John C. Brandt and Stephen P. Maran, *New Horizons in Astronomy* (San Francisco: W. H. Freeman, 1972).

Variable and double stars are discussed in depth in Lucien Rudaux and G. de Vaucouleurs, *Larousse Encyclopedia of Astronomy* (New York: Proemtheus Press, 1959).

Tips on observing variable and double stars have been compiled by Alan MacRobert in his "Backyard Astronomy" column in *Sky & Telescope*. See in particular the November 1984 and February 1985 issues.

For further information on the lore of star names, see Richard Hinckley Allen, *Star Names: Their Lore and Meaning* (New York: Dover, 1963).

Bausch & Lomb publishes a newsletter for users of their telescopes. The July/August 1986 edition of *Observer's Network* deals with double-star observing.

To get some of the flavor of a nineteenth-century sky guide, peruse T. W. Webb, *Celestial Objects for Common Telescopes* (New York: Dover, 1962; originally published in 1859).

An excellent survey of deep-sky objects is Kenneth Glyn Jones, *Messier's Nebulae and Star Clusters* (New York: American Elsevier, 1969).

For a discussion of Nadine Dinshaw's Polaris observations, see I. Peterson, "Catching Polaris during a Quick Change Act," *Science News* 137 (May 19, 1990): 309.

Additional information dealing with "unusual stars" can be obtained from:

George O. Abell, *Exploration of the Universe*, 3rd ed. (New York: Holt, Rinehart and Winston, 1975).

Donald H. Menzel and Jay M. Pasachoff, *A Field Guide to Stars and Planets*, 2nd ed. (Boston: Houghton Mifflin, 1983).

John Sanford, *Observing the Constellations* (New York: Fireside, 1989).

Chapter 7. To View the Sun—and the Dragon That Stalks It

Solar References and Notes

A number of good tips on solar viewing are included in David Allen and Carol Allen, *Eclipse* (Boston: Allen & Unwin, 1987).

For more technical solar information, a good textbook is John C. Brandt and Stephen P. Maran, *New Horizons in Astronomy* (San Francisco: W. H. Freeman, 1972).

For information on event-alert networks for amateur solar observers, see David A. Rosenthal, "Solar Alerts for the Amateur," in "Backyard Astronomy" column, conducted by Alan M. MacRobert, *Sky & Telescope* 79 (February 1990): 166–167.

For an introduction to video astronomy, see Alan W. Macfarlane, "A Primer for Video Astronomy," in "Observer's Page" column, conducted by Dennis di Cicco, *Sky & Telescope* 79 (February 1990): 226–231.

Eclipse References and Notes

A good semitechnical introduction to eclipse science is included in John C. Brandt and Stephen P. Maran, *New Horizons in Astronomy* (San Francisco: W. H. Freeman, 1972).

Eclipse folklore and history and information on eclipse photography are included in David Allen and Carol Allen, *Eclipse* (Boston: Allen & Unwin, 1987). Another good source for eclipse information is Donald H. Menzel and Jay M. Pasachoff, *A Field Guide to Stars and Planets,* 2nd ed. (Boston: Houghton Mifflin, 1983).

For consideration of ancient eclipses and application of Stonehenge as an eclipse predictor, see:

Gerald S. Hawkins, *Stonehenge Decoded* (Garden City NY: Doubleday, 1965).

Fred Hoyle, *On Stonehenge* (San Francisco: W. H. Freeman, 1977).

Chapter 8. Visitors in the Sky

Meteor References and Notes

A good introduction to the ancient history of the human interaction with meteors and meteorites is included in Gerald S. Hawkins, *Mindsteps to the Cosmos* (New York: Harper & Row, 1983).

For a colorful and authoritative introduction to the meteorite, see Kenneth F. Weaver, "Meteorites: Invaders from Space," *National Geographic* 170 (September 1986): 390–418. Of particular interest is the dramatic fortuitous color photo of the August 10, 1972, bolide that narrowly missed impacting Salt Lake City.

To plan scientifically serious meteor parties, refer to:

Grant Fjermedal, *New Horizons in Amateur Astronomy* (New York: Putnam, 1989).

Donald H. Menzel and Jay M. Pasachoff, *A Field Guide to Stars and Planets,* 2nd ed. (Boston: Houghton Mifflin, 1983).

Comet References and Notes

An excellent reference describing the Norman Conquest of Britain in 1066 and the influence of Halley's comet on the actions of contemporary Europeans is Christopher Hibbert, *Tower of London* (New York: Newsweek Book Division, 1971).

To review the historical background of comet observations and much more comet lore, consult Carl Sagan and Ann Druyan, *Comet* (New York: Random House, 1985).

More technical treatments of comet astronomy are included in many college-level textbooks. An excellent one is George O. Abell, *Exploration of the Universe,* 3rd ed. (New York: Holt, Rinehart and Winston, 1975).

A recent report on the progress of efforts to verify or disprove Professor Gold's unconventional theory is Richard A. Kerr, "When a Radical Experiment Goes Bust," *Science* 247 (1990): 1177–1179.

For information on comet photography, consult Donald H. Menzel and Jay M. Pasachoff, *A Field Guide to Stars and Planets,* 2nd ed. (Boston: Houghton Mifflin, 1983).

Experienced and very patient observers with a hankering for immortality might be interested in trying their hand at comet discovery. If they succeed, their names could be forever attached to the comet they discover. As described by Grant Fjermedal, *New Horizons in Amateur Astronomy* (New York: Putnam, 1989), ideal viewing conditions, high-quality equipment, and a good deal of persistence are essential for the successful comet hunter.

For more information on habitable comets, consult Freeman Dyson, *Disturbing the Universe* (New York: Harper & Row, 1979). More recent work on the concept is reviewed in Eugene Mallove and Gregory Matloff, *The Starflight Handbook* (New York: John Wiley & Sons, 1989).

Spacecraft References and Notes

A good, although slightly technical, introduction to the observation of artificial earth-satellites is W. Petri, "Artificial Earth Satellites," in G. D. Roth, ed., *Astronomy: a Handbook*, trans. from German by Arthur Beer (New York: Springer-Verlag, 1975), ch. 14.

A more mathematical treatment, including a satellite chronology to 1970, is Jean-Claude Pecker, *Experimental Astronomy* (New York: Springer-Verlag, 1970).

Some professional astronomers have been able to photograph *Mir* through their large reflectors. One of these photographs, taken through the Steward Observatory's 90-inch aperture reflector, clearly shows the bright solar panels of the space station and is reproduced in Grant Fjermedal, *New Horizons in Amateur Astronomy* (New York: Putnam, 1989).

Progress of the *Mir* missions is often reviewed in the publications of The British Interplanetary Society, particularly by correspondents including Neville Kidger in *Spaceflight*. Some *Mir* communication information is provided by John Branegan in *Spaceflight* 30 (1988): 108–112. A method of keeping track of this active spacecraft and predicting visible passes over the United Kingdom is also discussed by John Branegan in *Spaceflight* 30 (1988): 156–160.

Resources for the Urban Astronomer: To See Farther

This section describes various astronomical resources and how to tap into them. Proper utilization of these resources will prevent the budding astronomer from reinventing the wheel, so to speak. It is hoped that the interested urban astronomer will use this resources section to pursue his or her avocation in greater depth. Information on eclipse viewing expeditions, variable star and meteor viewing groups, and space age activities for the serious amateur urban astronomer is included.

Monthly Publications Devoted to Astronomy

For the adult reader, the best of these publications are *Astronomy* and *Sky & Telescope*. For the younger reader, an excellent monthly publication is *Odyssey*.

Monthly and Weekly Publications Containing an Astronomy Column or Astronomy Articles

Monthly star charts and discussions of sky events are included in *Natural History*. Articles dealing with astronomy often appear in *National Geographic, Omni, Science News, Discover, Smithsonian*

Magazine, and many other monthly publications. Major newspapers, especially *The New York Times* Sunday edition, publish weekly observable star maps. A nice feature of *Natural History* is the advertisements by travel agencies that regularly schedule eclipse observing expeditions on cruise ships and airliners.

Your Local Astronomy Club

Many cities have one or more astronomy clubs that conduct regular meetings, lectures, and observing sessions. Membership in such a club will introduce you to other astronomers whose assistance will prove invaluable. Although major clubs are sometimes listed in the pages of the major astronomy monthlies, you could also attempt to contact your local club through your city's planetarium, science museum, or universities. The Amateur Astronomers Association of New York, for example, conducts a series of scheduled lectures at the Hayden Planetarium, at the American Museum of Natural History.

National Organizations

Perhaps the best all-purpose astronomy organization for the amateur (or professional) astronomer is the Astronomical Society of the Pacific (ASP), which is located at 300 Ashton Avenue, San Francisco, California 94112. As well as publishing an excellent journal, *Mercury,* the ASP mails monthly star charts to members, conducts a series of seminars and meetings, and publishes more specialized material dealing with astronomical research and education. A number of other specialized national (and international) astronomy organizations exist. These include:

American Association of Lunar and Planetary Observers, P.O. Box 16131, San Francisco, California 94116

American Association of Variable Star Observers, 25 Birch Street, Cambridge, Massachusetts 02138

American Meteor Society, Department of Physics and Astronomy, State University of New York, Genesco, New York 14454

Central Bureau for Astronomical Telegrams, Harvard-Smithsonian Center for Astrophysics, 60 Garden Street, Cambridge, Massachusetts 02138

International Amateur–Professional Photoelectric Photometry, Dyer Observatory, Vanderbilt University, Nashville, Tennessee 37235

International Occultation Timing Association, P.O. Box 7488, Silver Spring, Maryland 20907

Resources for the Teacher

The teacher conducting planetarium lectures, skywatches, or astronomy classes should consider joining the International Planetarium Society (IPS), c/o Hansen Planetarium, 15 South State Street, Salt Lake City, Utah 84111. As well as publishing a periodic planetarium directory and conducting professional meetings, IPS also publishes a useful monthly, *The Planetarian.*

Other Publications

A number of annual almanacs devoted to astronomy in whole or in part are available. Foremost among these is *The Observer's Handbook,* which is published annually by The Royal Astronomical Society of Canada, in Toronto. Also of value is *The Air Almanac,* which is jointly published each year by the U.S. Naval Observatory in Washington, D.C., and Her Majesty's Stationery Office in London, U.K. Very many astronomical textbooks and books devoted to various aspects of amateur astronomy are also published each year. Among the best are those listed in the chapter references section of this book.

Space Age Activities

A space age activity open to the serious amateur astronomer is the possibility of submitting a winning proposal for observations with the newly launched Hubble Space Telescope (HST). Five proposals by amateurs were accepted from a group of about 200 proposals from 500 amateurs. A total of 17 hours of observing time on the orbiting facility will be devoted to the programs chosen. Future contributions by amateur groups will most likely be solicited for observing time on the HST and its successors. The best sources for information about such astronomical competitions are the monthly astronomical magazines and journals listed earlier. For a report on amateur use of the Hubble Space Telescope, see Stephen James O'Meara, "How Amateurs Will Use the HST," *Sky & Telescope* 79 (January 1990): 30–32.

Glossary of Astronomical Terms

Absolute magnitude: A comparative measure of stellar light intensity that is based upon only the star's luminous energy output, not its distance from the observer.

Altitude: The angular distance of a celestial object above the horizon. Altitude varies from 0 degrees for an object on the horizon to 90 degrees for an object directly overhead.

Aperture: The size of a telescope's primary lens or mirror.

Aphelion: The farthest distance an object in solar orbit gets from the Sun.

Apogee: The farthest distance an object in earth orbit gets from Earth.

Apparent magnitude: A comparative measure of stellar light intensity that is based upon both the star's intrinsic luminous energy output and its distance from the observer.

Apparition: The portion of a comet's orbit around the Sun when it is visible from Earth.

Asteroid: A minor planet. A rocky or metallic object tens to hundreds of miles in diameter orbiting the Sun. Most asteroids are usually confined to a belt between the orbits of the planets Mars and Jupiter.

Astrometric binary: A pair of gravitationally attached stars in which only one can be seen. The invisible member demonstrates its existence by affecting the motion of the visible star of the pair.

Astronomical unit: The average Earth–Sun separation (about 93 million miles).

Aurora: A beautiful optical phenomenon occurring in Earth's upper atmosphere usually at high latitudes. Auroras are caused by interaction between the solar wind and Earth's atmosphere.

Azimuth: The angular distance of an object from geographic north. A due east object is at 90 degrees azimuth; south corresponds to 180 degrees azimuth; west is 270 degrees azimuth.

Baily's beads: A phenomenon occurring during a total solar eclipse when sunlight passes through valleys in the lunar highlands.

Black hole: An object with such a high density that light and other radiation cannot escape from it.

Bolide: A very bright and sometimes audible fireball produced by an unusually large meteor or meteorite entering Earth's atmosphere.

Chromosphere: The lowest layer of the Sun's atmosphere.

Coma: A gaseous cloud surrounding the nucleus of a comet near perihelion.

Comet: An icy object orbiting the Sun. The comet's nucleus is less than 100 miles in diameter and consists of layers of rock over ice. Although usually orbiting the Sun at a distance of billions or trillions of miles, some comets are flung into elliptical orbits with perihelions so close that much of the ice melts to produce a dramatic tail. Because of solar radiation pressure, a comet's tail always points away from the Sun.

Conjunction: The condition of two celestial bodies that occurs when they have identical celestial longitudes.

Constellation: A familiar stellar pattern or configuration that is often named for a legendary or mythological individual.

Corona: The outermost layer of the Sun's atmosphere.

Earthshine: The dim light on the Moon's dark surface caused by sunlight refracted through Earth's atmosphere.

Eclipse: The condition that occurs when a celestial body blocks the light emitted by another celestial object.

Eclipsing variable star: A variable star in which the light variations are caused by a member of a binary occulting light from its companion.

Ecliptic: The apparent path in the sky followed by the Sun and naked-eye planets.

Elliptical galaxy: A galaxy with an elliptical (roughly egg-shaped) configuration.

Faculae: Bright regions visible near the solar limb.

Flare: An eruption of light and ionized particles from the Sun or another star.

Galaxy: A gravitational arrangement of billions of stars.

Gas giant planet: A planet type typified by dense atmospheres, many satellites, and ring systems.

Geocentric cosmogony: Obsolete world view placing a motionless Earth in the center of the Solar System with other planets and the Sun and Moon revolving around Earth.

Globular cluster: A tight collection of older stars located in a halo outside the plane of the Milky Way but gravitationally associated with our galaxy.

Great Red Spot: An atmospheric disturbance on the planet Jupiter that is easily viewed using a small telescope and that is larger than Earth.

Heliocentric cosmogony: Correct modern world view in which the Sun is the center of the Solar System and the planets (including Earth) revolve around the Sun.

Hertzsprung–Russell (H–R) diagram: A graph of stellar intrinsic luminosity or absolute magnitude versus surface temperature, color, or spectral class.

Inferior planet: A planet closer to the Sun than is Earth.

Ionosphere: An upper layer of Earth's atmosphere in which electrons have been stripped from atomic nuclei, which converts electrically neutral atoms into charged ions.

Kinetic energy: Energy of motion, often abbreviated as KE. Mathematically, KE is defined as one-half the product of an object's mass and the square of its velocity.

Light-year: The distance traveled by light in one year (63,240 astronomical units).

Magnetosphere: A region above Earth's atmosphere that is still influenced by Earth's magnetic field.

Main sequence: A band on the H–R diagram that contains most stars. Main-sequence stars tend to be stable hydrogen-burners like the Sun.

Mare: A flat plain on the Moon. Some features on Mars have also been dubbed as maria (plural).

Meteor: A "shooting star." A short-lived streak in the night sky usually caused by ice particles from a comet's tail entering Earth's atmosphere.

Meteorite: An object from space that survives passage through Earth's atmosphere and reaches the ground. Usually a chunk of rock from the asteroid belt.

Nadir: The point in the sky directly on the other side of Earth from an observer's position.

Nebula: An interstellar or intergalactic collection of gas or dust.

Neutron star: A very high-density star composed entirely of neutrons.

Oort cloud: A diffuse cloud of perhaps trillions of comets that is located 20,000 to 50,000 astronomical units from the Sun.

Open cluster: A collection of young stars in the plane of the Milky Way Galaxy.

Opposition: The condition of two celestial bodies that occurs when their celestial longitudes differ by 180 degrees.

Optical binary: Two stars that are really quite distant from each other but appear to be close together because of chance alignment of the lines of sight from Earth to the stars.

Penumbra: The partial-shadow region and least darkest portion of a sunspot.

Perigee: The closest approach to Earth of an earth-satellite.

Perihelion: The closest approach to the Sun of a planet, comet, or asteroid.

Photosphere: The visible disk of the Sun.

Planet: An object that shines by reflected light and circles a star.

Posigrade motion: The usual "positive" motion of a planet in the sky.

Potential energy: Energy of position, often abbreviated as PE. For an object at a height above Earth's surface much smaller than the Earth's radius, PE is the product of the object's weight on the surface and its height above the surface.

Precession: The conical shift of Earth's pole through a 26,000-year cycle.

Prominence: A bright region of hot gas extending from the Sun's chromosphere up into the solar corona.

Radiant: The sky position from which the tracks of meteors in a meteor shower seem to originate.

Red giant: A very large and luminous, cool, red star.

Reticle eyepiece: A telescope eyepiece equipped with an internal calibration that allows the observer to measure the angular extent or separation of celestial objects.

Retrograde motion: The occasional "backward" motion of a planet, now known to be caused by the relative motions of the planets and Earth around the Sun.

Revolution: The motion of a satellite around a planet or a planet around the Sun.

Rotation: The spin of a planet around its axis.

Saros: An 18.61-year eclipse cycle that has been known since ancient times.

Satellite: An object that shines by reflected light and circles a planet.

Sidereal period: The time required for a celestial object to complete one orbit, measured against the stars.

Solar wind: The variable stream of ionized particles emitted from the Sun into the inner Solar System.

Spectroscopic binary: A double star whose members cannot be directly observed but manifest their existence in photographs of the star's spectrum.

Spiral galaxy: A disk-shaped galaxy like our Milky Way.

Star: A celestial object, such as our Sun, that shines by self-generated radiation.

Stratosphere: A layer of Earth's atmosphere that is above the troposphere and below the ionosphere. An ozone layer in the stratosphere absorbs much of the ultraviolet radiation from the Sun reaching Earth's outer atmosphere.

Sungrazer: A comet in a very elongated elliptical orbit with a perihelion very close to the Sun. At least one sungrazer has been observed by a spacecraft to actually be destroyed as it rammed the photosphere.

Sunspot: A portion on the visible disk of the Sun (photosphere) that appears darker because it is slightly cooler than the surrounding material.

Supergiant star: A very large, highly luminous star.

Superior planet: A planet more distant from the Sun than is Earth.

Synodic period: The time required for a celestial object to complete one orbit, measured against the Sun.

Terminator: The line separating dark and sunlit portions of the Moon's or a planet's disk.

Troposphere: The lower layer of Earth's atmosphere. Most of Earth's weather is in the troposphere.

Umbra: The total-shadow region and darkest portion of a sunspot.

Visual binary: A gravitationally attached binary star in which both members can be seen by the naked eye or through a telescope.

White dwarf: The final state of a star of roughly solar mass. A dim, small object that has exhausted its store of thermonuclear fuel.

Zenith: The point in the sky directly over the observer's head.

Zodiac: A belt of 12 constellations on or near the ecliptic.

APPENDIX 1

Observer's Ephemeris for the Naked-Eye Planets Visible from a Mid-Latitude (43 Degrees) Northern Hemisphere City

PLANET LOCATION (ZODIACAL CONSTELLATION)
BETWEEN 1991 AND 2000

Date (Time = 1 Hour after Local Sunset)	Venus	Mars	Jupiter	Saturn
Jan. 15, 1991	—	Taurus	Cancer	—
Mar. 15, 1991	Ari/Pis	Gem/Tau	Cancer	—
June 15, 1991 (Note A)	Cancer	Cancer	Cancer	—
Sept. 15, 1991	—	—	—	Capricorn
Jan. 15, 1992	—	—	—	—
Mar. 15, 1992	—	—	Leo	—
June 15, 1992	—	—	Leo	—
Sept. 15, 1992	—	—	—	Capricorn
Jan. 15, 1993	Aquarius	Gemini	—	—
Mar. 15, 1993	Pisces	Gemini	—	—
June 15, 1993	—	Leo	Virgo	—
Sept. 15, 1993	—	—	—	Cap/Aqr
Jan. 15, 1994	—	—	—	Aquarius
Mar. 15, 1994	—	—	—	—
June 15, 1994	Cancer	—	Libra	—
Sept. 15, 1994 (Note B)	—	—	Libra	Aquarius
Jan. 15, 1995	—	—	—	Aquarius
Mar. 15, 1995	—	Cancer	—	—
June 15, 1995	—	Leo	Scorpio	—
Sept. 15, 1995	—	—	Scorpio	Aqr/Pis

(continued)

NOTE: Use with Star Charts in Appendix 6.

189

(continued)

Date (Time = 1 Hour after Local Sunset)	Venus	Mars	Jupiter	Saturn
Jan. 15, 1996	Aquarius	—	—	Aqr/Pis
Mar. 15, 1996	Aries	—	—	—
June 15, 1996	—	—	—	—
Sept. 15, 1996	—	—	Sagittarius	Pisces
Jan. 15, 1997	—	—	—	Aqr/Pis
Mar. 15, 1997	—	Leo/Vir	—	—
June 15, 1997	—	Leo/Vir	—	—
Sept. 15, 1997 (Note C)	—	Libra	Capricorn	—
Jan. 15, 1998	—	—	Aquarius	Pisces
Mar. 15, 1998	—	—	—	—
June 15, 1998	—	—	—	—
Sept. 15, 1998	—	—	Aqr/Pis	—
Jan. 15, 1999	—	—	Aqr/Pis	Pisces
Mar. 15, 1999 (Note D)	Ari/Pis	—	—	Ari/Pis
June 15, 1999 (Note E)	Cancer	Virgo	—	—
Sept. 15, 1999 (Note F)	—	Scorpio	—	—
Jan. 15, 2000 (Note G)	—	Aquarius	Ari/Pis	Aries
Mar. 15, 2000 (Note H)	—	Pisces	Aries	Aries
June 15, 2000	—	—	—	—
Sept. 15, 2000	—	—	—	—

Source: All tabulated planetary data was obtained using the Atari Planetarium, copyright 1979, Deltron Ltd., 155 Deer Hill Road, Lebanon, New Jersey 08833. The computer used was an Atari 1040ST microcomputer.

Venus, Mars, Jupiter, and Saturn have sidereal periods of 225 days, 687 days, 11.9 years, and 29.5 years, respectively. Venus, the most rapidly moving of the easily observable naked-eye planets, will change houses of the zodiac every 20 days or so. For the other planets, the predictions in the table are fairly accurate for intermediate dates.

When a planet lies on or near the cusp of two constellations, abbreviations have been used. These are as follows: Aqr (Aquarius), Ari (Aries), Cap (Capricorn), Gem (Gemini), Pis (Pisces), Tau (Taurus), and Vir (Virgo).

Notes
Note A: Venus, Jupiter, Mars, and the crescent Moon are all about 15 degrees above the western horizon. These objects are all within a span of about 10 degrees.

Note B: Marginal for urban observing; Jupiter is only about 8 degrees above the southwestern horizon.

Note C: Marginal; Mars is only about 9 degrees above the southwestern horizon.

Note D: Venus and Saturn are separated by about 4 degrees (8 lunar diameters).

Note E: Venus is about 10 degrees above the crescent Moon.

Note F: Mars is about 10 degrees from the crescent Moon.

Note G: Saturn is very close to the gibbous Moon.

Note H: Saturn, Jupiter, and Mars are in an essentially straight line with a length of about 24 degrees. Saturn is 31 degrees above the western horizon; Jupiter is 24 degrees above the horizon; Mars is about 14 degrees above the western horizon.

APPENDIX 2

Some Major Northern Hemisphere Meteor Showers

ANNUAL METEOR SHOWERS AND RELATED COMETS

Name (Constellation)	Date	Time	Associated Comet	Meteors per Hour
Lyrids (Lyra)	4/21	11 P.M.	1861 I	15
Eta Aquarids (Aquarius)	5/4	2 A.M.	Halley	20
Delta Aquarids (Aquarius)	7/28	5 A.M.	—	20
Perseids (Perseus)	8/11	8 P.M.	1862 III	50
Orionids (Orion)	10/21	Midnight	Halley	25
Leonids (Leo)	11/17	7 A.M.	1866 I	15
Geminids (Gemini)	12/13	7 P.M.	—	50

Sources: George O. Abell, *Exploration of the Universe,* 3rd ed. (New York: Holt, Rinehart and Winston, 1975); Donald H. Menzel and Jay M. Pasachoff, *A Field Guide to Stars and Planets,* 2nd ed. (Boston: Houghton Mifflin, 1983).

Notes

Source comets, when known, have been listed. Comet 1866 I is the first comet discovered in 1866.

The number of meteors per hour is an average for a sky in which magnitude 6 stars are visible. Generally, a smaller number of meteors will radiate from the shower radiant a few days before or after the dates listed.

Meteor Triangulation

With the aid of high school trigonometry and Figure A–1, an equation for the height of a meteor can easily be derived. Two observing stations are assumed; the angles of elevation for the simultaneously observed meteor track are A and B. Height H is the perpendicular line to the horizontal distance D between the two stations. The two right triangles are denoted as I and II, and X is the distance between angle A and the base of H. The equation for determining H is

$$H = \frac{D \, \text{Tan} \, (A) \, \text{Tan} \, (B)}{\text{Tan} \, (A) \, + \, \text{Tan} \, (B)}$$

In this equation, "Tan" represents the tangent of the appropriate angle. The equation also works if the meteor track is not between the two stations. If the meteor is directly over one of the stations—say, station 2—the equation will reduce to the form

$$H = D \, \text{Tan} \, (A)$$

Figure A–1 Use of triangulation to determine a meteor's height

193

APPENDIX 4

Lunar Eclipses Visible in North, Central, and South America, the Atlantic Ocean, and Europe (1991–2000)

DATES AND LOCATIONS FOR LUNAR ECLIPSES

Date	Comments	Area of Visibility
Dec. 21, 1991	Partial	North America
June 15, 1992	Partial	Central and South America
Dec. 10, 1992	Total, 74-min. max. dur.	Brazil, Europe
Nov. 29, 1993	Total, 50-min. max. dur.	Western hemisphere
May 25, 1994	Partial	South America
Apr. 4, 1996	Total, 84-min. max. dur.	Europe, South America
Sept. 27, 1996	Total, 72-min. max. dur.	Western hemisphere
Mar. 24, 1997	Partial	Western hemisphere

Source: David Allen and Carol Allen, *Eclipse* (Boston: Allen & Unwin, 1987).

APPENDIX 5

Solar Eclipses Visible in North, Central, and South America, the Atlantic Ocean, and Europe (1991–2000)

DATES AND LOCATIONS FOR SOLAR ECLIPSES

Date	Comments	Area of Visibility
July 11, 1991	Total, 414-sec. max. dur.	Central America, Brazil
June 30, 1992	Total	South Atlantic
May 10, 1994	Annular, 374-sec. max. dur.	North America, Atlantic
Nov. 3, 1994	Total, 263-sec. max. dur.	Brazil, Peru, South Atlantic
Apr. 29, 1995	Annular, 398-sec. max. dur.	Brazil, Peru, South Atlantic
Feb. 26, 1998	Total, 236-sec. max. dur.	Panama, North Atlantic
Aug. 11, 1999	Annular, 143-sec. max. dur.	England, Central Europe, North Atlantic

Source: David Allen and Carol Allen, *Eclipse* (Boston: Allen & Unwin, 1987).

APPENDIX 6

Seasonal Star Charts

The seasonal star charts were composed with the assistance of a star finder manufactured by Saga Industries in Saugatuck, Connecticut. The operation of each chart is described below the chart. Easily recognized star groupings are identified. The constellations of the zodiac are denoted in boldface on each chart. The zodiacal constellations correspond with the following abbreviations: Aqr (Aquarius), Ari (Aries), Can (Cancer), Cap (Capricorn), Gem (Gemini), Leo (Leo), Lib (Libra), Pis (Pisces), Sag (Sagittarius), Sco (Scorpio), Tau (Taurus), and Vir (Virgo).

The star charts will approximate the evening sky for mid-northern latitude locations. More sophisticated star finders are marketed by most large planetariums and science centers. Used in conjunction with the planetary data in Appendix 1, these star charts can be used to locate naked-eye planets (except Mercury) between 1991 and 2000.

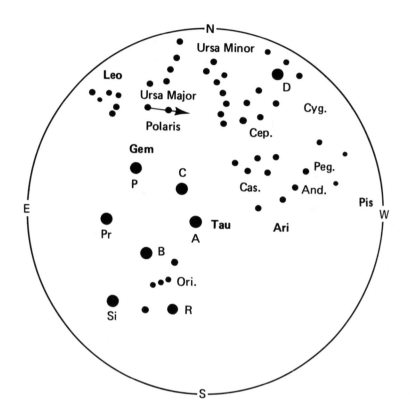

Constellations:

Ursa Major
Ursa Minor
Cassiopeia (Cas.)
Cepheus (Cep.)
Cygnus (Cyg.)
Andromeda (And.)
Pegasus (Peg.)
Orion (Ori.)
Leo

Bright Stars:

A: Aldebaran in Taurus
B: Betelgeuse in Orion
C: Capella in Auriga
D: Deneb in Cygnus
P: Pollux in Gemini
Pr: Procyon in Canis Minor
R: Rigel in Orion
Si: Sirius in Canis Major

Note: Hold overhead with N toward the north. Letters E, S, and W on the horizon will line up with east, south, and west directions. Notice the pointer from the Big Dipper (Ursa Major) to the North Star, Polaris. Four stars in Pegasus and Andromeda resemble a box. Cassiopeia is like a *W*, and Cepheus resembles an upside-down house. Orion the Hunter is easy to recognize by the three stars in his belt.

Figure A-2 Winter evening skies—best for 6 P.M., February 20; 8 P.M., January 20; and 10 P.M., December 20

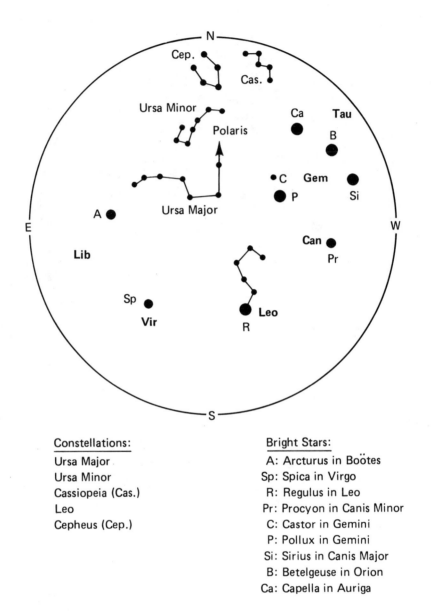

Constellations:

Ursa Major
Ursa Minor
Cassiopeia (Cas.)
Leo
Cepheus (Cep.)

Bright Stars:

A: Arcturus in Boötes
Sp: Spica in Virgo
R: Regulus in Leo
Pr: Procyon in Canis Minor
C: Castor in Gemini
P: Pollux in Gemini
Si: Sirius in Canis Major
B: Betelgeuse in Orion
Ca: Capella in Auriga

Note: Hold overhead with N toward the north. Letters E, S, and W on the horizon will line up with east, south, and west directions. Notice the pointer from the Big Dipper (Ursa Major) to the North Star, Polaris. Leo's head resembles a sickle, and Cassiopeia is like an inverted *W*. By following the "arc" of the end stars in the handle of the Big Dipper, you can easily find the bright red giant Arcturus. Cepheus resembles an inverted house low in the north.

Figure A–3 Spring evening skies—best for 7 P.M., May 20; 9 P.M., April 20; and 11 P.M., March 20

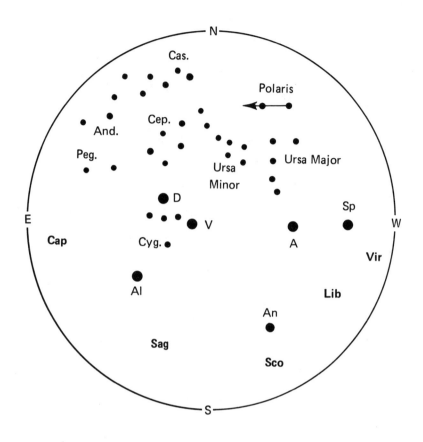

Constellations:
Ursa Major
Ursa Minor
Cassiopeia (Cas.)
Cepheus (Cep.)
Andromeda (And.)
Pegasus (Peg.)
Cygnus (Cyg.)

Bright Stars:
A: Arcturus in Boötes
An: Antares in Scorpio
Al: Altair in Aquila
D: Deneb in Cygnus
Sp: Spica in Virgo
V: Vega in Lyra

Note: Hold overhead with N toward the north. Letters E, S, and W on the horizon will line up with east, south, and west directions. Notice the pointer from the Big Dipper (Ursa Major) to the North Star, Polaris. Four stars in Pegasus and Andromeda resemble a box. Cygnus the Swan resembles a bird; Cassiopeia is like an inverted *W*; and Cepheus resembles a house.

Figure A-4 Summer evening skies—best for 7:30 P.M., August 20; 9:30 P.M., July 20; and 11:00 P.M., June 20

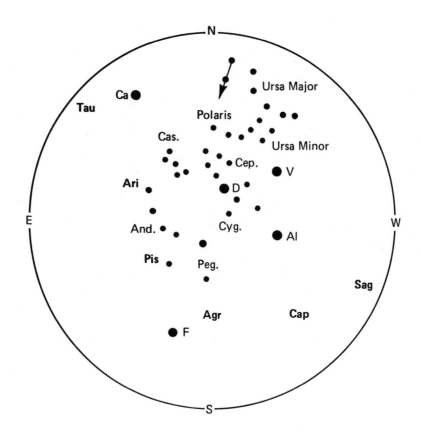

Constellations:
Ursa Major
Ursa Minor
Cassiopeia (Cas.)
Cepheus (Cep.)
Andromeda (And.)
Pegasus (Peg.)
Cygnus (Cyg.)

Bright Stars:
Al: Altair in Aquila
Ca: Capella in Auriga
D: Deneb in Cygnus
F: Fomalhaut in Pisces Australis
V: Vega in Lyra

Note: Hold overhead with N toward the north. Letters E, S, and W on the horizon will line up with east, south, and west directions. Notice the pointer from the Big Dipper (Ursa Major) to the North Star, Polaris. Four stars in Pegasus and Andromeda resemble a box. Cygnus the Swan resembles a bird; Cassiopeia is like a *W*; and Cepheus resembles a house.

Figure A–5 Autumn evening skies—best for 6 P.M., November 20; 8 P.M., October 20; and 10 P.M., September 20

APPENDIX 7

Stellar Evolution and the Hertzsprung–Russell Diagram

Figure A–6 presents a Hertzsprung–Russell (H–R) diagram and a portion of the evolutionary track of a star like the Sun. The Sun initially "lights up" as a cool *red giant* and follows the track labeled (1) toward the *main sequence.* Approximately 30 million years are required for a solar-mass star to contract to the main sequence.

After 10 billion years of main-sequence stability, the Sun will expand once more along track (2). The Sun has another 5 billion years or so to burn before it will leave the main sequence. The duration for track (2) is approximately half a billion years.

Next, after a period of instability, the Sun will move more or less horizontally to position (3). Various types of stellar variability may occur as the star evolves between points (2) and (3). Then, the star moves vertically downward to point (4) and finally contracts to become an incredibly dense *white dwarf* of planetary dimensions.

The stellar spectral classes (O, B, A, etc.) are further subdivided into subclasses of decreasing surface temperature. Class A, for example, is divided in tenths: A0, A1, A2, etc. The Sun is classified as a G2 main-sequence dwarf.

Sources: Robert Jastrow and Malcolm H. Thompson, *Astronomy: Fundamentals and Frontiers* (New York: John Wiley & Sons, 1972); Patrick Moore, *Astronomers' Stars* (New York: Norton, 1989).

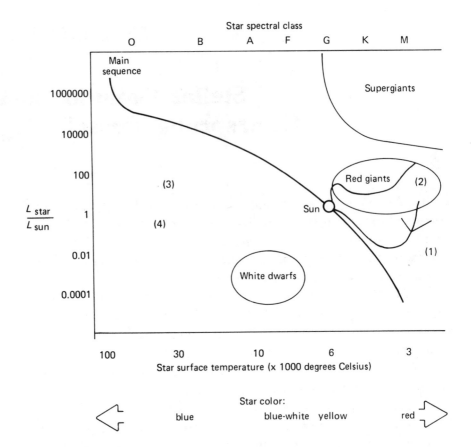

Figure A-6 Hertzsprung–Russell (H–R) diagram: Stellar luminosity (*L*) is plotted versus stellar spectral class and surface temperature. Positions (1), (2), (3), and (4) are various evolutionary stages for the Sun

APPENDIX 8

Star Magnitudes

The idea of a relative measure of star brightness, or stellar magnitude, goes back to at least the second century B.C. when Hipparchus compiled a list of roughly 1,000 stars and divided them somewhat arbitrarily into six brightness categories. After the development of early means of quantifying star brightness, Norman R. Pogson suggested a more mathematically precise modification to the earlier scale.

We can get a good idea of the workings of quantitative magnitude scales by considering the dimmest stars that are visible to the unaided human eye during ideal seeing conditions. These are visual apparent magnitude 6 stars. When we go up one step in brightness to visual apparent magnitude 5, the amount of light that reaches our eye from the brighter star is actually about 2.5 times greater than that from the dimmer one. Similarly, the eye receives about 2.5 times more light from a magnitude 4 star than it does from a magnitude 5 star and about 6.25 times more light from a magnitude 4 star than from a magnitude 6 star.

For mathematically inclined readers, the magnitudes between two stars (M_1 and M_2) are related to the light received from the two stars, or the luminous fluxes (L_1 and L_2):

$$M_1 - M_2 = 2.5 \log_{10} \frac{L_2}{L_1}$$

In translation, this formula states that the magnitude difference between the two stars is equal to the base-10 logarithm of the ratio of luminous fluxes.

Source: George O. Abell, *Exploration of the Universe,* 3rd ed. (New York: Holt, Rinehart and Winston, 1975).

As well as visual apparent magnitudes, there are photographic apparent magnitudes and corresponding magnitudes for a wide variety of sensors sensitive in different spectral ranges. The absolute magnitude system removes distance as a factor in a star's brightness by mathematically moving all stars considered to the same calibration distance (32.6 light-years from Earth). Astrophysicists are more interested in absolute magnitudes than in apparent magnitudes because this system depends upon the intrinsic differences among stars, not their relative positions from Earth.

Bright Stars Visible in the Northern Hemisphere

BRIGHT STARS

Star Name	Constellation	Apparent Visual Magnitude	Spectral Class	Notes
Sirius	Canis Major	−1.5	A1V	wd
Arcturus	Boötes	−0.1	K2III	
Vega	Lyra	0.0	A0V	
Capella	Auriga	0.1	GIII	m1
Rigel	Orion	0.1	B8I	m2
Procyon	Canis Minor	0.4	F5V	wd
Betelgeuse	Orion	0.4	M2I	
Altair	Aquila	0.8	A7V	
Aldebaran	Taurus	0.9 [0.8–0.9]	K5III	m3,v
Spica	Virgo	0.9 [0.9–1.0]	B1V	v
Antares	Scorpio	0.9 [0.9–1.0]	MII	v
Pollux	Gemini	1.2	K0III	
Fomalhaut	Pisces Australis	1.2	A3V	m4
Deneb	Cygnus	1.3	A2I	
Regulus	Leo	1.4	B7V	m1
Castor	Gemini	1.6	A1V	m5

Sources: George O. Abell, *Exploration of the Universe,* 3rd. ed. (New York: Holt, Rinehart and Winston, 1975); Donald H. Menzel and Jay M. Pasachoff, *A Field Guide to Stars and Planets,* 2nd ed. (Boston: Houghton Mifflin, 1983); Ruth J. Northcott, ed., *The Observer's Handbook 1968* (Toronto, Ontario: Royal Astronomical Society of Canada, 1968).

Notes
Stars are listed in order of decreasing brightness. All magnitudes have been rounded off to the nearest tenth.

wd: white dwarf companion

m1: has two much dimmer companions

(continued)

m2: attended by a much dimmer class B companion

m3: has a much dimmer class M2 companion

m4: attended by a much dimmer class K companion

m5: consists of three spectroscopic binaries

v: variable star; median magnitude and magnitude variation (in brackets); Spica is an eclipsing variable (4-day period); Aldebaran may be irregular; Antares is classified as semiregular.

Luminosity classes are included as I through V after spectral classes: I (supergiant); II (bright giant); III (giant); IV (subgiant, intermediate between giant and main sequence); V (main sequence).

Some Easily Observable Variable Stars (in Order of Decreasing Brightness)

VARIABLE STARS

Star	Type of Variable	Visual Magnitude		Period (Days)	Spectroscopic Variation or Types
		Max.	Min.		
Alpha Orionis	Semiregular	0.1	1.2	2070	M2
Beta Aurigae	Eclipsing	2.1	2.2	3.96	A1–A1
Beta Persei	Eclipsing	2.2	3.4	2.87	B8–G4
Delta Orionis	Eclipsing	2.5	2.6	5.73	B1–B2
Alpha Ursa Minoris	Cepheid	2.6	2.8	3.97	F7–F9
Alpha Herculis	Semiregular	3.1	3.9	131	M4
Rho Persei	Irregular	3.2	4.1	—	M
Zeta Geminorum	Cepheid	3.7	4.1	10.15	G
Delta Cephei	Cepheid	3.6	4.3	5.37	F4–G6
Eta Aquilae	Cepheid	3.7	4.4	7.18	F2–G9
Lambda Taurui	Eclipsing	3.8	4.1	3.95	B3–K2

Source: Lucien Rudaux and G. de Vaucouleurs, *Larousse Encyclopedia of Astronomy* (New York: Prometheus Press, 1959).

Notes
Some of these stars are better known by their popular names. Alpha Orionis is Betelgeuse; Beta Aurigae is Sharatan; Beta Perseis is Algol, the Demon Star; Alpha Ursa Minoris is Polaris, the North Star; Alpha Herculi is Ras Algethi. For more information on stellar names, consult Richard Hinckley Allen, *Star Names: Their Lore and Meaning* (New York: Dover, 1963).

To be included in the above table, a star's maximum brightness is brighter than magnitude 4 and the star is at all times visible to the unaided human eye.

For the semiregular variables listed, the mean pseudo-periods are presented. These are the most recognizable periodic variations of the stars' complex light curves.

APPENDIX 11

Some Easily Observable Binary Stars

BINARY STARS

Star	Separation (Seconds of Arc)	Magnitudes and Colors
Beta Cygni	34	3.2 orange, 5.4 blue
Eta Persei	28	3.9 orange, 8.7 blue
Zeta Ursa Majoris	14	2.4 white, 4.0 white
Eta Cassiopeiae	11[a]	3.7 yellow, 7.4 red
Gamma Andromedae	10	2.3 gold, 4.8 blue
Beta Orionis	10	0.3 white, 9.0 blue
Gamma Virginis	5[a]	3.7 yellow, 3.7 yellow
Alpha Herculis	5	3.5 red, 5.4 green
Gamma Leonis	4	2.6 yellow, 3.8 yellow
Alpha Scorpii	3	1.2 red, 7.0 green
Alpha Geminorum	2[a]	2.7 white, 3.7 white

Sources: Lucien Rudaux and G. de Vaucouleurs, *Larousse Encyclopedia of Astronomy* (New York: Prometheus Press, 1959); Alan M. MacRobert, "Observing Double Stars," in "Backyard Astronomy" column, *Sky & Telescope* 78 (November, 1984): 417–419.

Notes
Those stars with angular separations marked by superscript "a" revolve comparatively rapidly around their common center of mass. The separations are therefore quite variable for these pairs.

Alpha Geminorum, with a separation of about 2 seconds of arc, can be easily resolved in a telescope of 3-inch aperture. To resolve the components of Alpha Herculis, with a separation of 5 seconds of arc, a 2-inch aperture telescope is more than ample. Binoculars will resolve the pairs with separations 10 seconds of arc or greater.

Stars selected for this table are easily visible to the naked eye from a Northern Hemisphere location and belong to one of the major constellations.

Common names for some of the binaries listed are Albireo for Beta Cygni, Mizar for Zeta Ursa Major, Almach for Gamma Andromeda, Rigel for Beta Orionis, Ras Algethi for Alpha Herculis, Antares for Alpha Scorpii, and Castor for Alpha Geminorum. For more information regarding the evolution of star names, consult Richard Hinckley Allen, *Star Names: Their Lore and Meaning* (New York: Dover, 1963).

APPENDIX 12

Photographs of the Sky—Pointers for the Beginner

Sooner or later, most amateurs will desire to attempt to photograph those celestial objects that are most dramatic through the lenses and mirrors of their telescopes. Instead of duplicating information that has been gleaned from the century-long labors of a legion of astrophotographers, this section simply outlines some of the basic requirements for the success of your initial photographic experiments.

First of all, you will need a good telescope equipped with an equatorial mount and a clock drive. You should align the mount as accurately as possible with geographical north, center the object within the field of view, turn on the clock drive, and then expose the film.

For instruments of equal aperture, a refractor produces superior photos compared to those of a Newtonian reflector and a Newtonian is superior to a Cassegrain. Best results for the Moon, the planets, and double stars are obtained by using the method of eyepiece projection. That is, using a special adaptor, the camera is mounted behind the eyepiece and any filter that is used. Other camera mounting arrangements are superior for deep-sky objects.

An oft-recommended camera is a 35-mm SLR (single lens reflex) with a detachable lens. High-definition, high-resolution film is required to capture detail. Atmospheric seeing should be steady. The best photos are often produced during the winter when skies

Sources: Rick Dilsizian, "High-Resolution Lunar and Planetary Photometry," *Astronomy* 16, no. 1 (January 1988): 70–77; P. Clay Sherrod and Thomas L. Koed, *A Complete Manual of Amateur Astronomy* (New York: Prentice-Hall, 1981); Richard Talcott, "Tools for the Astrophotographer," *Astronomy* 16, no. 1 (January 1988): 78–81.

are less turbulent. Your telescope should be stable, and the drive mechanism must be steady during the duration of the exposure. Also, you must carefully check the focus and be very careful not to shake the telescope–camera combination during the exposure. More vibration will be experienced on a windy night than on a calm one.

When a celestial object is close to the horizon, it passes through a larger amount of atmosphere (or air mass) than when it is close to the zenith. To reduce the influence of atmospheric effects ("twinkle"), it is a good idea to photograph objects when they are as close to the zenith as possible.

Proper exposure time is also an important factor. The proper exposure time depends upon the object being photographed, film speed, and the optical system of your camera and telescope. Consult the sources listed for more details on the determination of exposure time.

A Primer on Photoelectric Photometry

Photometry can be defined as the quantitative measurement of light. The human eye is a crude photometer. With training, you can learn to estimate a star's brightness to 0.2 magnitude; the luminous flux received from it, to about 20 percent. This is done by visually comparing the star under observation to reference stars of known visual apparent magnitude that are near it in the sky.

If you observe an astronomical photograph of stars of various photographic apparent magnitudes, you will immediately discover that the dimmer stars are approximately pointlike. Photographic images of the brighter stars tend to be overexposed and smeared out into a circular disk. One means of estimating photographic magnitudes (to an accuracy of 0.1 or so) is to carefully measure the size of the overexposed disk in a stellar exposure.

Photoelectric photometry, in which light photons are electronically converted into electrons, allows astronomers to measure apparent star magnitudes to an accuracy of 0.01 magnitude or less. You will not be able to do as well from a murky urban site, but accuracies of 0.1 magnitude are certainly obtainable.

The operation of any photoelectric device can be summarized as follows. Light from the object under study is first directed

Source: P. Clay Sherrod and Thomas L. Koed, *A Complete Manual of Amateur Astronomy* (New York: Prentice-Hall, 1981).

More technical sources: Jean Dufay, *Introduction to Astrophysics: The Stars,* trans. from French by Owen Gingerich (New York: Dover, 1964); William A. Hiltner, ed., *Astronomical Techniques* (Chicago: Univ. of Chicago Press, 1962); Gregory L. Matloff, "Monitoring Stratospheric Ozone and Aerosols Using Orbiting Photoelectric Detectors," *Journal of the Astronautical Sciences* 24 (1976): 365–382; G. D. Roth, ed., *Astronomy: A Handbook,* trans. from German by Arthur Beer (New York: Springer-Verlag, 1975).

through an appropriate filter and then on to an electronic device that applies the photoelectric effect to convert light energy into electron energy. A number of amplification stages are then used to increase the energy of the electrons, which ultimately appears on a strip-chart recorder or digital meter as a voltage or current reading. Most of these devices are very linear. Over a wide range of stellar apparent luminosities, the light received from the star is directly proportional to the reading on the output device.

Solid-state, video, and electron-tube photometers are utilized by astronomers. So that photometric measurements taken of the same object by observers in different locations can be compared, great efforts have been expended to arrive at common photometric systems. One popular system is the UBVRI system, in which filters and photomultiplier tubes are used to obtain data in a near-ultraviolet (or U) spectral band, a visible blue (or B) band, a yellow visible (or V) band, a red-infrared (or R) band, and a near-infrared (or I) spectral band.

To measure a star's photometric filter magnitude, you wait until the subject star is as high in the sky as it will get during the observing session. Then, you activate the photometer (which has been previously attached to the telescope's eyepiece) and record the recorder or meter reading corresponding to the star under observation. To compensate for the brightness of the urban evening sky, you then drive the telescope–photometer combination so that it is pointing at a portion of the night sky slightly off the subject star. This is called the *background reading*. The luminous flux received from the star is equal to the difference between the two readings.

You should then repeat the process for one or more reference stars located as close to the subject star in the sky as possible. Since the filter magnitudes of the reference stars are well documented, this process allows you to calibrate your meter or recorder readings in terms of filter magnitudes.

To reduce the effects of the atmosphere, which reduces the luminous flux received from a star and consequently increases the star's apparent magnitude, you should select reference stars as close to the subject star in the sky as possible. Because these atmospheric extinction effects are highly dependent upon color and increase as the star descends toward the horizon, you should select reference stars as close as possible to the subject star in terms of location and spectral class.

You could use astronomical photoelectric photometry to measure atmospheric extinction and therefore the conditions of the local atmosphere. Such long-term extinction data, carefully reduced and documented and archived for a period of time, can be useful to local environmental groups considering air pollution.

To perform atmospheric extinction studies, a star of spectral class AOV is often selected. By definition, these blue-white main-sequence dwarfs, with surface temperatures of 11,000 degrees Celsius or so, are of identical filter magnitude no matter what spectral band you observe with.

The favorite AOV dwarf for most Northern Hemisphere atmospheric extinction studies is Vega. The third brightest star in the northern sky, Vega passes very close to the zenith during summer evenings. Best of all, the apparent magnitude of Vega is zero, or very close to zero, in all magnitude systems.

You must commit a good deal of your evening to an extinction study. It is best to observe the star as its altitude above the horizon varies. If you start observing at 9 P.M. on the night of August 30, for example, you will observe Vega near its highest point in the sky. By 2 A.M., you will most likely have lost the star in the glare of the urban sky near the horizon.

In tabulating extinction data, it is very important to include time as well as apparent star brightness because the star's altitude is a function of time. Usually, extinction data is plotted following the method of Bouguer. Apparent star magnitude is plotted versus *air mass*. The air mass is defined as the secant (the reciprocal of the cosine) of the zenith angle. A star that is directly overhead has a zenith angle of 0 degrees. One on the horizon has a zenith angle of 90 degrees.

The air mass of a star directly overhead is 1. After constructing the linear plot of apparent magnitude versus air mass, you can extrapolate to the zero air mass magnitude, or the apparent magnitude of the subject star above the atmosphere. For Vega, once again, this magnitude is zero or close to zero whether you are concerned with visual, photographic, or photoelectric filter magnitudes.

If you are mathematically inclined, you may wish to plan near-simultaneous observations of the same star with different spectral-band filters. Such an approach allows an astronomer to isolate the effects of selected contributors to atmospheric extinction (see Matloff source cited above).

Index

Index

astrology, 8,29

astronomical coordinate systems, 51–52

Astronomical Society of the Pacific, 53

astronomical software, 60

astrophotography, 47, 75–80

Audobon Society, 20

aurora, 133

azimuth, 51

B

Babylon, 7

Baily, Francis, 145

Baily's Beads, 145

binoculars, 41, 50, 67, 103, 162

black hole, 14, 107, 124

bolide (fireball), 152

Brahe, Tycho, 8, 84

British Columbia, University of, 111

Bronze Age, 7

Burroughs, Edgar Rice, 91

C

calendar, 6, 29

carbon dioxide, atmospheric, 15

celestial equator, 9, 52

celestial north pole, 29–30, 52

celestial south pole, 52

celestial sphere, 52

Chaldeans, 8

clock drive, 47, 128

clouds, 15, 23, 66

comet(s), 64, 85, 155–163

    artificial, 165–166

    belt (Oort Belt), 159–160

    colonization, 161

    forested, 161

    as "hairy stars", 155

    in history, 155–157

    hydrocarbons from, 159

    impacts and mass extinctions, 158

    long–period, 159–161

    lore and mythology, 156–157

    observations, 162

    probes, 161

    short–period (periodic), 155

    storms, 157–159

    sungrazers, 161

comets, particular

    Austin, 161

    Halley's, 155

    Kohoutek, 161

comets, parts of

    coma, 161

    hydrogen cloud, 157, 160–161

    nucleus, 157, 160

    tail, 156–157, 160–161

compass, use of, 51, 129

constellations, northern circumpolar, 31

constellations, northern-hemisphere-seasonal, 30

    autumn, 34–35

    spring, 36–37

    summer, 37–38

    winter, 35–36

constellations, particular

    Andromeda, 31, 35–36

    Aquila, 31, 33, 35, 38

    Aquarius, 30–31

    Aries, 30

    Auriga, 31, 33, 35

    Big Bear (see Ursa Major)

    Boötes, 31, 38

    Cancer, 30, 124

    Canis Major, 31, 35–37

    Canis Minor, 31, 35–37

    Capricorn, 30

    Cassiopeia, 30, 34–38

    Cepheus, 30, 34, 38

    Cetus, 113

Index